Inspiring !
June 2008

MIRACLES
and Amazing Messages

WHEN MIRACLES HAPPEN
True Stories of God's Divine Touch

Edited by Mary Hollingsworth

Guideposts
New York, New York

Acknowledgments

Every attempt has been made to credit the sources of copyrighted material used in this book. If any such acknowledgment has been inadvertently omitted or miscredited, receipt of such information would be appreciated.

All material that originally appeared in Guideposts publicatons is reprinted with permission. Copyright © Guideposts. All rights reserved.

Unless otherwise noted, Scripture quotations are from the New Century Verson®. Copyright © 1987, 1988, 1991 by Thomas Nelson, Inc. All rights reserved. Quotations designated KJV are from the King James Version of the Bible. Quotations designated NASB are from the New American Standard Bible, © 1960, 1977 by the Lockman Foundation. Quotations designated NIV are from The Holy Bible, New International Version. Copyright © 1973, 1978, 1984, International Bible Society. Used by permission of Zondervan Bible Publishers. Quotations designated RSV are from the *Revised Standard Version of the Bible*, copyright © National Council of Churches of Christ in America. Used by permission.

"The Night Francine Left for College," " A Woman of Faith," "Through Tiny Windows," "Rainy Day Soup," and "Searching Normandy" published by permission from *Whispers from Heaven*, copyright © 2001, 2002 Publications International, Ltd. ""Miracle Child" and "Naturally Supernatural" found in *I Am With You Always* by G. Scott Sparrow (New York: Bantam, 1995). "The Voice of an Angel" and "A Transformation of the Spirit" found in *Angels: The Mysterious Messengers* edited by Rex Hauck (New York: Bantam, 1993).

"A Note Out of the Blue" by Mary Hollingsworth, "An Unexpected Touch of Grace" by Robert L. Wise, "A Miracle of Song" and "True Poetry in Motion" by Elizabeth Schmeidler, "Don't Ask My Wife to Pray for You" and " A Tiny Handful of Promise" by Norris Burkes, "A Book and a Bond" by Lisa Allred, "Angels on the Freeway" by Pat J. Sikora, "Peanut Butter and Crackers" by Saundra Kay, "The Legacy of Prayer" by Holly Baxley, "Something Extra" by Linda Wright, "A Delightful Message" by Sue Ferguson, "My Greatest Thanksgiving" and "Startled by a Silent Word" by Nancy B. Gibbs, "The Treasure" by Joanna Gaines, "I Come to the Garden Alone" by Christine E. Collier, "The Tattooed Stranger" by Susan Farr Fahncke, "The Message of Bubbles, Flowers, Raindrops, and Leaves" by Betty Beaver Cantwell, "Wright is Right" by Anita Wadley, "Logic Doesn't Change God's Plans" by Isabel Wolseley Torrey, "The Miracle Bibles" by Ron Wheeler and "Message Imprinted on a Heart" by Kate R. Thomas; are used by permission of the authors.

Editorial, research, and content development managed by Shady Oaks Studio, Bedford, Texas. Team members: Patty Crowley, Rhonda Hogan, Mary Hollingsworth, Mary Kay Knox, Kathryn Murray, Nancy Sullivan, Stephanie Terry, and Barbara Tork.

www.guideposts.org
(800) 431-2344
Guideposts Books & Inspirational Media Division
Illustrations by Ron Bucalo
Jacket design and photo by The DesignWorks Group, Inc.

Printed in the United States of America

Contents

CHAPTER 2 YOU'VE GOT MAIL!

CHAPTER 3 WHILE YOU WERE OUT

CHAPTER 4 A FRIENDLY REMINDER

〰〰

*C*HAPTER 5   MIRACLE MESSAGES

Introduction

Amazing messages from God—they come to us in surprising ways, with life-changing news and at times we least expect them. Sometimes they come out of the blue with no warning at all and take our breath away. Sometimes they come in the mail, over the phone, through a friend, or in mysterious ways we can never explain or totally comprehend. But however they come and whenever they arrive, there's no doubt that they are from God. No other explanation makes sense.

Many people would like to confine God's messages to an arena that's definable, predictable, explainable, like the Bible. And while the Bible is certainly the greatest treasure trove of messages from God we know, God can simply not be stuffed between the pages of a Book and pressed down for safekeeping like a fall leaf. He is omnipotent and omnipresent—all powerful and everywhere at once. So, like Him, His messages are divine, unpredictable, and unexplainable at times—in other words, miraculous!

In *Miracles and Amazing Messages*, you'll find a fascinating collection of true stories about how God delivers special messages to His people and how those messages transform their lives.

In Chapter 1, "Out of the Blue," God adds his own ethereal note to the song Infinity is recording. Becky is surprised by the voice of an angel. And God uses Deputy Police Chief Robert Rabe to save several hostages from dangerous gunmen.

Kathryn is reminded in Chapter 2 that "You've Got Mail" when an envelope from her friends holds a wonderful message from God for her. Lisa gives a book to a new friend and discovers a surprising bond that they share. And when Pat's car breaks down, she meets angels on the freeway.

When Saundra is down to peanut butter and crackers for her family, God answers her prayer for food in a surprising way in Chapter 3, "While You Were Out." Catharine answers the $32,000 question with God's help and receives exactly what she needed. And Joyce takes God's Word into the public classroom, even though everyone said it couldn't be done.

In Chapter 4, "A Friendly Reminder," Joanna's loss of a precious treasure becomes God's message to save a friend. Susan and her children deliver God's unbiased love to a heavily tattooed stranger. And Betty's Down syndrome son shows us how to delight in God's love through soap bubbles and raindrops.

In "Miracle Messages" from God in Chapter 5 Ron

finds two thousand Spanish Bibles—exactly what he needs for his planned mission trip to Guatemala. Nancy is startled by an encounter with a silent world. And Melissa finds God's peace when her husband, Chris, dies . . . but continues to live!

Perhaps, after reading these stories, you'll begin to hear and see the special messages God is sending to you in unique and loving ways too. After all, He's your Father, and fathers like to communicate with their children. Come with us now into the miracles and amazing messages of God.

MARY HOLLINGSWORTH

MIRACLES
and Amazing
Messages

CHAPTER 1

Out of the Blue

"I have heard a message from the LORD" (Jeremiah 49:14).

Have you ever received an amazing message out of the blue? It just comes out of nowhere it seems. Good news. Bad news. Surprising news that turns your world upside down . . . or sets it right side up again. Whatever the end result, these messages out of the blue may be God just trying to get our attention. So when they come, listen up!

Showdown on Wisconsin Avenue

ROBERT RABE

It is 12:15 Tuesday afternoon, November 16, 1976, and I have just settled down to some police paperwork. But I never get to finish it. I look up to see a station clerk rush into my office. "Chief, communications has just notified us of a hostage situation in Georgetown."

Hostage. One of the toughest. Desperate criminals holding innocent people as pawns. Too often in my twenty-six years of police work have I heard of cases where victims have died amid a flurry of gun shots or were executed by enraged captors.

But the hostage situation is one that my Special Operations officers are trained to cover. The Georgetown case is now our responsibility.

In minutes I'm in a squad car roaring up M Street toward this picturesque area of high-fashion shops and nineteenth-century residences. As we race along I radio our barricade team into action. From the dispatcher I learn that several gunmen have invaded a men's boutique on Wisconsin Avenue; they've already fired at policemen ar are now holed up inside the shop holding an undetermined number of hostages. One wounded officer has been rushed to the hospital.

As we careen onto Wisconsin Avenue I see the flashing red lights of scout cars and a crowd of people. The air is electric with tension. An officer points to the shop in a two-story brick building. It's impossible to see into the interior through a small display window filled with clothing. The building is quiet, ominous, like a time bomb about to explode.

Our barricade team van pulls up, and now the regular policemen who have been covering the building can get back to controlling the crowd and traffic.

We evacuate all surrounding buildings and set up a command post. Our team, fourteen highly trained men in bullet-resistant jackets and helmets and armed with rifles and shotguns, quietly take up stations around the building. Others position themselves on adjoining roofs where they wait with telescopic-sight rifles. But I pray that not one of them will be fired.

God loves everyone in that building. Can they be saved?

Our aim is to reach the leader inside the shop and establish some kind of communication with him. In a way, a situation like this is finding yourself in a fiery disagreement with someone. I have learned that if you can just communicate with your antagonist, there is hope of peaceful settlement.

But there has to be an atmosphere of mutual trust. Someone has to take the first step, and that someone has to be us. The alternative is exploding tempers, broken communication and, all too often in these situations, death and carnage.

If I can talk with my opponent this afternoon on a one-to-one basis, let him know I understand his situation and offer feasible alternatives, we'll have a better chance of saving lives.

Can I do this with the desperate men inside the shop? Their emotions are fast boiling to the danger level and I must reach them immediately. Bull horns or loudspeakers won't do. The men inside the shop might choose some hysterical response designed to impress the onlookers. Communication must be in an atmosphere of quiet.

An officer rushes up with the shop's phone number. Good! I leap into a street phone booth, ransacking my pockets for change. Calls are twenty cents and I have no dimes. I shove in a quarter and dial.

Busy.

I wait a moment, fingers drumming the scarred metal shelf. I try again. Still busy. Why? I stick my head out the door. "Phone's tied up!" I exclaim.

An officer's face flushes. "It's the press," he barks. "Radio and news reporters found the number and are interviewing the gunmen over the air. You can hear them on the radio now."

The media! How can anyone prevent the media from

giving enormous publicity to potential killers and inter-fering with our negotiation efforts without jeopardizing freedom of the press? It's an agonizing question. I cer-tainly don't have any easy answers.

But what will this do to the one-to-one rapport I want to establish? I can only try again. I shove in a quarter; this time my call goes through. Someone picks up the phone, slams it down.

Sweat beads on my forehead. I put the quarter back in. This time a male voice growls: "Who's this?"

"Deputy Chief Rabe of the Metropolitan Police Department."

The phone vibrates with searing obscenities.

"Who am I talking to?" I ask, forcing my voice into calmness. I have found people respond to the way in which they're addressed. If I speak calmly, maybe he'll simmer down. "If I know your name," I add, "we can talk better."

"James," he barks. "It's me and two others with hostages." He speaks in staccato bursts. I let him talk. If I can show this man I want to understand him, it will be half the battle. If the rage in his mind cools, he'll begin to think more clearly. My ultimate goal is that he will eventually realize the hopelessness of his situation and give himself up. But now he's still raging.

"Listen, you lousy cop," he shouts, "I come out with a hostage, you give me a car, then the other two guys with me will give themselves up. You clear the area, I get out of here and my hostage goes free."

Before I can respond he hangs up. I step out of the booth into the pale November sun. Now that he has made his demand, we'll wait a few minutes.

I learn that the men are holding six hostages. Nearby, the shop owner talks to two officers. He says there are four tailors and two women clerks inside.

Fifteen minutes pass. A police cruiser pulls up; it has a phone in it. Good, no more scrambling for change. I climb in and dial the shop. The gunman answers my ring instantly. "Hey, man, where's the car?" His voice has hysteria in it.

"I've got to work on that . . ."

He cuts me short. "Listen, I'm going to shoot one of the hostages and throw him out the front window if you don't get me that car now!"

Anger floods me. Who does he think he is, giving me orders? "Lord," I pray silently, "help me stay cool."

"Look," I answer softly, "you'll only get hurt yourself that way."

"I'm going to be killed anyway," he retorts.

"No, you won't," I say. "Nothing will happen to you unless I give the order." I want to convince him that I'm in charge, that he can trust me, negotiate with me.

"Yeah?" he fairly screams. "Well, you listen to me . . . I just smashed the nose of the man with me with my pistol and I'll put a bullet through his head if I don't get that car now!"

The line goes dead. Suddenly it's very hot in the

squad car. I sit there, holding the silent phone, sick inside. *Have I lost him? Should I get him a car?* I wonder. I decide against it. But what if he goes through with his threat?

An awesome weight sinks me deep into the seat cushion. The clamor outside the squad car rises. A newsman beats at the window, trying to talk to me. Police struggle to hold back the crowd. A malevolent force seems to fill the atmosphere. It would be so easy to have my team rush that building. Maybe the gunmen would be too frightened to kill the hostages.

No. I take hold of myself. We're here to save lives, not take them. Something infinitely more powerful than the malevolence fills me as I remember that the One really in charge here is a God of love and life, not death and destruction. If we continue to try to save lives, then we'll have His power with us. I remember St. Paul's words: "If God is for us, who can be against us?" (Romans 8:31 NIV).

Another newsman slips through the barricade toward me. I escape into a nearby bookstore, where the proprietor leads me to a small office with a phone. Now it's 1:15 P.M. Five times I dial the store; five times it's busy. I relax for a moment. I dial once more. James answers.

"Where's that car?" he demands. Is his voice a little less strident? "I'm not fooling around," he continues. "I got guns. Sure, you got guns and helicopters. But I got the hostages."

I try to visualize what he looks like as we talk. He sounds young. I listen, trying to put myself in his place.

"Look, James," I answer calmly, "I want to settle this whole thing as much as you. But you know I can't give you one of those marked police cars. Where would that get you?"

I present him questions, trying to keep him thinking. The more I can get him to the point of making logical decisions, the more hope we have.

"Believe me," I assure him, "We don't want you or anyone else to get hurt."

He hangs up, but now I sense I have someone on the other end of the line who wants to talk, not fight.

I glance at my watch. An hour has gone by. I take a deep breath. We have passed a crisis point. If someone loses his head, it's usually in the first hour.

Some good news arrives. The officer who was shot is all right; the bullet glanced off his leather belt. Then suddenly an aide rushes in to report that five hostages have slipped out of an unguarded basement exit. One gunman, obviously frightened, has come out with them and is in custody.

But the situation is now confused. We were told there were six employees. Is there still one hostage inside the shop? We question the owner. "It could be the other woman clerk," he stammers, "but . . . but now I'm not sure if she came to work this morning."

We put him on the phone to call her home or any other number she may be at. Fifteen minutes later he locates her in another part of the city.

I lean back in my chair. *Thank You, God.* That means there are just two gunmen in the building. But we must be careful. People can still get hurt.

At 2:45 P.M. we talk to James again. He's quieter now. Almost calm. Finally he says he'll give up.

He and his companion are ordered to throw their guns out the window, then come out the front door one by one with their hands on their heads, sliding down the steps on their backs.

Now I'm back out on the street watching. It's quiet. Finally, the door opens and the two men come out as ordered. They are both young, with many years left to them. Perhaps, if they try, those years can become good years.

As I watch, I think about what has happened. Eight human beings have lived through an explosive situation without getting hurt. I thank God once more for helping me stay cool. As long as people can communicate with one another, miracles can happen. What does the Bible say? "Come now, and let us reason together" (Isaiah 1:18).

By 3:15 P.M., the crowd has drifted away and traffic again moves down Wisconsin Avenue. I get into a police cruiser alone and drive around for a while. The paperwork on my desk can wait until morning.

A Note Out of the Blue

MARY HOLLINGSWORTH

Several years ago my a cappella Christian jazz ensemble called Infinity was recording a collection of twenty wedding songs for a Christian publishing house in Texas. We had been in the studio for several different sessions, and the project was nearing completion when a mysterious thing happened.

There were eight singers in Infinity—two on each voice part: soprano, alto, tenor, and bass. At times we broke into as many as eight different notes in harmonies that were complex and intricate, producing an exciting, close-harmony jazz sound—not an easy feat in pure a cappella (unaccompanied). So the album was considered quite unique.

The last song we recorded was entitled "Household of Faith." Various ones in the group had recorded solos during the sessions, and this happened to be my solo piece. So I was in a separate recording booth from the rest of the group. We could all see and hear each other, but my voice was put on a separate track so it could be reworked, if necessary.

"Household of Faith" begins quietly, but as it comes to the end it builds to a wonderful, huge climax—one of those places where we divided into several different notes. This time, though, in listening to the playback of the recording, our director heard an extremely high note that was not written in the music. It was an ethereal note that fit perfectly into the chord and was exciting to hear; it just wasn't in the music.

Our lyric soprano was Debra, but when the director asked her if she hit the note—she was the only logical one that could—she said no. Charlotte, our mezzo soprano and the director, knew she hadn't sung the note. And it was much too high for any of the rest of us. So where had it come from?

The studio engineer and Charlotte began going through each separate voice track to find the note. But it could not be heard on any of the eight individual tracks. And yet, when the engineer played all eight tracks together, once again the extra note was there as clear as a bell.

This time we all sat in the engineer's booth and listened for the note on each individual track. It simply was not there. But it came through gloriously when the tracks were played together. It was amazing!

Was it an overtone? Perhaps. That happens sometimes when a chord is in perfect tune. But we chose to believe that it was a message of blessing from God on the work we had done to His glory. Maybe an angel just added a heavenly touch to the song to show His approval—a note out of the blue, you might say. We like to think so. And today that note can still be heard clearly on the recorded song.

Miracle Child

G. SCOTT SPARROW

I am now a grandmother, age sixty-two. For many years I never spoke of my Christ experience. I wish now that I had looked up records so today I could have the proof nonbelievers seem to need. Somewhere I know there is some proof in hospital and church records, as I was called the Miracle Child.

Today I can't remember the dates. I was eleven years old (in Ohio). My mother, brother, and I had scarlet fever; my fever escalated and caused spinal meningitis.

My parents had lost everything. My father, a carpenter by trade, had been unemployed for a long time. The state of Ohio paid my hospital bills, even flying in a doctor from Chicago. The part of Ohio State University Hospital that I was in was a building apart from the main hospital with a high fence around it. I don't remember going in, but I remember my father carrying me out.

I remember one of the nine times that I was held in a tight ball and told not to move, as a big needle was put in my spine. Later, looking in a mirror, for years I could see and count these nine marks. I remember the horrible pain, and my thin, twisted legs.

My parents were told my death would be a terrible, screaming thing; best for them not to see or hear, to go home. I lost my sight and hearing but before that, saw my parents, grandparents and Reverend John Lang standing in the doorway of my room, not permitted to come in. The smiles, the thrown kisses, the waving good-bye, I remember and then the sea of pain.

Later, after losing my eyesight, I was lying on my right side. I heard a voice behind me say, "L. B., turn over." I said, "No, it hurts too much to move. You come around to this side of the bed." Then the voice said, "I promise you it will not hurt—turn over." Turning, I saw Jesus. I remember no other words Jesus said to me, yet I know we talked. I watched His beautifully-shaped hand reach out and touch my leg.

Sometime later, I remember remarking to a nurse about what pretty red hair she had. She looked at me in shocked surprise and rushed from the room. The room soon filled up with doctors asking questions. I was a very shy person and there were too many doctors, too many questions. I had to talk about this to Reverend Lang. He was the one person in all the world I wasn't too shy to talk to.

Reverend Lang listened, asked questions, and took many notes. I couldn't see the face of Christ, as it was like looking into a light bulb. But His clothes, the color and material, I had never seen—all that I can remember. I was very blond with very pale skin—the skin of Christ was much darker. The color of a piece of His hair I saw fall on His left shoulder as He reached out His left hand to touch me was a color I had never seen. Reverend Lang called it auburn.

My parents were told I could not live—I did. I was set in a chair and heard I would never walk—I did. They were told I never would have children—I had three.

I had not seen Reverend Lang for years when I saw in a local paper he was to speak at a church nearby. My sister and I were late so we slipped in a side door. Reverend Lang was speaking about a little girl, "a miracle child," he had known, who had seen and was healed by Christ. Here he was telling hundreds of people of the thing that had happened to me—the things we had talked about long ago.

A Coroner's Report

JANIS AMATUZIO

I'm a forensic pathologist. My job is understanding the cause of death, but it's also to speak for the dead. For more than a decade—since 1993 as coroner for Anoka County, Minnesota—I've been doing everything in my power to answer one question: how did this person die? Then I explain it to family members, physicians, law enforcement, and the courts. Often, death is a riddle.

I'm also a doctor, and like all doctors, a healer. How could a person who spends her time examining the deceased call herself a healer? Well, I'll tell you.

I come from a medical family. My dad is an internist and, growing up, I tagged along with him on house calls, watching him solve the mysteries of his patients' illnesses. He practiced medicine like the country doctor you see in old movies: worn leather medical bag, stethoscope draped around his neck and a big, reassuring smile that said, "Talk to me. I'll listen." Same with Mom, a nurse. Watching the difference the two of them made in people's lives, it was only natural that I'd go into medicine myself. In no other job did a love for knowledge and a love for people meet so perfectly.

It was Dad who suggested forensic pathology. He recognized my excitement over finding answers—my insatiable curiosity about how the human body works. "You'd be a doctor's doctor," he told me. "It's the basis of all medicine. Nothing teaches you more about life than death."

I liked the idea of discovering the cause of death. There is no more intimate possession than the body itself. Performing an autopsy, I don't see an anonymous corpse in front of me, but the evidence left behind of that person's soul: an open book telling me about how he or she lived. If well and decently, that's evident in a thousand different ways. If badly, that's evident too. A life story is visible right there in the organs. You can tell the choices people made in life.

I am passionate about my work. My autopsy reports are the last word on my patients. Each one is a new challenge, a new mystery, and I can't rest easy until I've made sense of it. I'm not at peace with a case until I've discovered exactly how the person I'm examining has passed on.

Eventually an idea formed in my mind. What about the families? If knowledge really heals, why not share the knowledge I gained in my autopsies? Why not personally tell them the cause of death? Nothing in life hurts as much as losing a loved one. Maybe talking to me could help ease the family's grief, perhaps even help in the healing process. I called the next of kin whenever possible and shared my knowledge of how their loved one had died. In almost every case it helped them.

It helped me, too, fulfilling my desire to be a healer, like Mom and Dad. I opened myself up to the survivors' pain, grief, and anger, as well as their hope and gratitude. And something more . . . more than I could ever have imagined.

Take Julie Carson, the wife of a man named Randy on whom I performed an autopsy. She'd come home one day to find Randy dead on the floor next to his easy chair, the TV remote still in his hand. In the left ventricle of Randy's heart I discovered a large tumor that penetrated the main chamber. I suspected the tumor had played a part in Randy's death and called in a specialist to help interpret the evidence. The tests took weeks, which delayed the death certificate. Julie was left waiting, alone with her grief. In seventeen years she and her husband hadn't spent a single night apart. How could God have taken him away from her? And so suddenly, without even a chance to say one last "I love you."

I called Julie the minute the report was ready. She wanted to know everything. "The growth in your husband's heart was benign," I explained. "But a piece of it broke off and entered one of his coronary arteries. The tumor fragment plugged the vessel, just as a blood clot would have. In essence, Randy died of a heart attack."

Julie was silent for a moment. "Did he suffer?" she asked. I told her that, in my opinion, Randy had slipped away painlessly.

"With his favorite toy in hand," she said, her voice softening. "I usually got into bed while Randy was still watching TV, channel-surfing mostly. But I never shut my eyes till I heard him coming up the stairs. Can I tell you something, Dr. Amatuzio?"

I thought of my dad, who always had time to listen. "Of course," I said.

"After Randy died, I couldn't sleep. Then something happened. One night I finally drifted off. Footsteps in the hall woke me. I just knew it was Randy. Sure enough, he walked right into our bedroom, sat down next to me, and took my hand. We talked about the kids, our finances, the house. 'Our love is forever,' he said. 'Just think of me and I'll be there.' I know our love still connects us, Doctor."

You might think this story is a rarity. But the fact is, over the years I've heard scores of stories like it. They've opened me to a whole other world: the one that lies beyond the borders of death. Having grown up in the church, I understood the concept of an afterlife. Yet how amazing it was to confront it as a doctor!

Mary Bare was the mother of a young man named Greg, who'd died in an auto accident. I called Mary after conducting his autopsy and asked if she had any questions. Her first one was the same as Julie's: "Did he suffer?" In this case as well, I was able to tell Mary that, in all likelihood, Greg hadn't suffered.

Mary seemed almost to expect that answer. "Dr. Amatuzio," she said, "can I tell you something?" When Greg was a boy he had a favorite babysitter named Sheila. She was Mary's favorite, too, because she had a special knack for comforting him. Shortly after Greg's death, Mary called Sheila.

"Sheila told me," Mary said, "that on the night Greg died, she had been awakened by a loud voice saying 'Hey, Sheila!' "

Sheila sat up and saw Greg—all grown up—standing next to her bed. He was very distraught that his death had caused such pain and sadness. Sheila didn't stop to question whether she was dreaming. She did what came naturally and comforted him, just as she had done so many times when he was a boy.

A few nights later Sheila was awakened again—this time by a gentle light filling her bedroom. Again, Greg stood at the foot of her bed. But this time there was no more confusion, no more sadness about him. "Tell Mom I'm okay now," Greg said. It seemed that Greg's life was going on, in a new world where he was at peace. Sheila was relieved to get Mary's call. It was confirmation that she should relay this message of comfort sent from God to a grieving mother.

Yet sometimes people do come back from the dead. I was having lunch one day with several law enforcement officials, including a local sheriff—a shrewd and highly respected man. People had heard about my interest in the subject, and somehow the conversation took that turn. The sheriff spoke up. "Dying's not the big deal people make it out to be. I drowned once." I looked at him. He didn't say "almost drowned," he said "drowned."

The sheriff had grown up on a lake. My brothers and I spent just about every day of the summer swimming there and carrying on. We used to dive off the lifeguard tower and race to touch the bottom."

But that got too easy. The sheriff and his brothers added a new twist to the game. The tower's legs were ladders, the rungs of which started out wide and got narrower toward the top. He and his brothers would weave back and forth between the rungs as they made their way up. One day, just a few feet from the surface, the sheriff got stuck. "I looked up and saw that my brother had made it to the surface," he said. "I panicked. Then I blacked out." The sheriff came to in a rescue boat after mouth-to-mouth resuscitation.

"Do you remember anything from when you were unconscious?" I ventured.

The sheriff looked down. Something in his face changed. "Why, yes," he said. "I do. I don't usually talk about it, but it's as clear as if it were yesterday. I remember thinking *I'm going to die.* I took in a large gulp of water, and all of a sudden, I was up above my body, looking down on it. There were beautiful colors everywhere. I felt sorry for my body, but I wasn't worried about it. There was all sorts of activity. My brothers and the lifeguard were there. But I felt perfectly calm and found myself speeding along above the surface of the water toward someplace so near yet so perfect I never could have imagined it. Then, all of a sudden, I was jolted back into my body."

The sheriff said that what he remembered most was that when he came back from the stunningly vivid world he'd entered for a moment, everything in the regular world looked dull—as if he'd gone from a color movie to one in black and white.

"You know, Doc," the sheriff said, looking at me with a twinkle in his eye, "I know that you're the coroner and see this stuff every day. You know that it bothers a lot of folks. But I'm not afraid of death. Not after what happened to me."

Can I explain all of these stories I've heard, in the way that I can explain exactly why a body I examine died in the way it did? Probably not. We are not meant to see the soul. Yet I have come to believe that these experiences reveal the truth of what I believe: Dying is part of a larger picture, a moment of transformation on a path of eternal life. Discovering the cause of death opens the door to a grander reality. We don't end when our bodies give out. In a life full of solving mysteries, that's the greatest one I've discovered—the mystery of the soul.

The Voice of an Angel

BECKY HOBBS

One December, a couple of weeks before Christmas, I started getting premonitions that I would be in a bad car accident. They would hit me when I'd lie down to go to sleep, at that stage when you are just drifting off. All of a sudden, *boom!* there would be this big crash and I'd sit straight up in bed sweating, with my heart pounding wildly. And I'd have this awful feeling of despair, like, "But I'm not ready yet; it's not my time to go. I have more things to do." This kept going on for a couple of weeks before Christmas. A friend of mine and I were driving back to Oklahoma to see my mom for the holidays, and we had to pull over a few times because my heart would start pounding. As a result, we got in really late on Christmas Eve, and I had to tell my mom, "I'm sorry we're so late, but I just keep having this feeling I am going to be in a bad car wreck and it won't leave me alone." And she understood.

Well, we had Christmas and drove back to Nashville, and nothing happened. So in Nashville I thought, *Wow, it's over. It wasn't meant to be; it didn't happen.* Well, it wouldn't l let up.

Almost every night afterward, that feeling would happen. My birthday is January 24, and in the wee hours of that morning, I was in the kitchen making some goodies for my party; I was going to have some folks over that night. And I had this feeling of somebody tugging on my sleeve, taking hold of my arm to take me out to my front yard. And it was something I didn't have a choice about; it was something I had to do. I thought, *What is going on?* because it was three o'clock in the morning! I looked up at the stars, and I got goosebumps, and I asked, "What do you want me to know? What are you trying to tell me?" And this loud, booming voice—it was as loud as any physical voice I've ever heard—said, "Be careful, this may be your last birthday." The voice in the front yard was so commanding I was just shaking in my boots. But I knew the voice, and I was not afraid of it; the voice loved me. The voice was here to help me and cared about me.

That is all the voice said. And I knew right then that the warning was associated with the premonitions I'd been having about being in a car accident. The key word for me was "may." This *may* be your last birthday. So I thought, *Then it's up to me. I have to be aware. I have to be careful. I'm in a dangerous situation right now.* After that I tried to ask for more information, but that's all the information I could get. The message had been given and that was all I was allowed to hear. So I went back in the house and that night had my birthday party.

The very next day, January 25, I got into my van with my band and drove to Albertville, Alabama, to play for a police benefit. We loaded up our equipment and were on our way back to the hotel to pick up our things before driving on to Nashville. We were at a four-way intersection on the highway and it was raining and dark.

I was sitting in the back of the van—on the left-hand side in the third seat. I looked out to the left and saw an eighteen-wheeler barreling toward the intersection. I thought, *My God, he's not going to be able to stop.* And then I looked over and at that moment our light turned green. Randy was driving the van, and I felt his foot lift off the brake and the car start going. And I knew right then. *Boom!* It was that feeling, the same feeling I'd been having every night, that feeling of, "I'm not ready yet. I'm not ready yet to go."

I yelled at Randy. I yelled for him to stop and he did. The eighteen-wheeler slid into us. We were pulling a trailer and I don't know how many times we spun around. The collision totaled the van—a Dodge Maxivan. And then there was quiet. I didn't know if I was dead or alive, because I couldn't feel anything. We were shaken up pretty badly, and at that moment I thought, *Well, either I'm out of my body or I'm okay.* And

I really didn't know for a couple of minutes. We were bruised, we were cut, but everybody got out of it alive. And I feel that the warning from the angel saved all our lives because a split second later we would have been completely broadsided. The truck slid into us, but it hit the left front of the van, which is the strongest part. The state trooper said, "You are lucky because you all would have been killed if it was a split second later." We would have been broadsided and, I am sure, killed. The truck was going too fast.

It took me awhile to look back and be able to realize that the voice I had heard all those times was an angel. I always thought you have to see an angel; now I realize you can hear angels. The voice was my guardian angel, and ever since then I know those of us who are here are here for a reason or we would not be here. The very fact that we are still here means we have not fulfilled our purpose here on Earth. And I think the angels are with us right now, because it is their number-one thing to help us on this planet. And for those of us who are communicating with angels, it is our number-one thing right now to spread the word and to help others. And that's what I am trying to do.

An Unexpected
Touch of Grace

ROBERT L. WISE

B ill Cole didn't appear to be a person who struggled
with spiritual emptiness. Athletic, and muscular, I
had seen Bill around the gym. With his red hair flying in
all directions, I had watched him press an enormous
amount of weight. Of course, I didn't know Bill Cole
then, but he appeared to be a strong man.

For most of my adult life, I worked out in a gym to
keep myself in good physical condition. While I wasn't
interested in looking like a body-builder, I had learned
the value of staying fit. Early in my ministry, infection
from acute nephritis caused my kidneys nearly to stop
functioning. Most of the congregation wasn't sure if I
was going to make it. I finally reached the point where I
was sleeping twenty hours a day, fighting urinary poi-
soning and experiencing double vision. My personal
physician couldn't find a way to stop the illness.

Prior to the advent of the Charismatic Movement, I

had never been around healing experiences and knew nothing about the subject. However, at the lowest moment of my illness, I had a remarkable experience of the healing power of Jesus Christ. Unsolicited and unexpected, the restorative power of the Resurrection surged through my body and I overcame the disease overnight. I had no idea what had occurred, but I was glad to be alive and not sleeping twenty hours a day.

My physical struggle had taught me how important it is to take care of myself. However, I was mystified by what had happened to me and began studying the healing ministry. Much to my surprise, I found that the healing work of Jesus Christ never stopped. Every century brought people with the ability to bring healing. Slowly, I became aware there were concepts for teaching healing just as there were for evangelism or education and they could be communicated. As the years went by, I taught people in churches all over America, South America, and in the Far East how to minister to the sick and dying.

One of the insights that I took away from this time was that staying in good health was better than recovering from sickness. Exercise and physical exertion had proved to be of major importance in keeping my body running. My training efforts kept me running on the right course.

One particular evening I decided to grab a quick workout before I rushed on to perform a wedding ceremony. I thought pumping a little iron would be energizing before I headed for the church. I settled in for a few repetitions on a hack squat machine that exercise my thigh muscles. Slanted at an angle, the device allowed me to handle a great deal of weight by only slightly pushing the weights up and down at an angle with my legs. As long as I didn't go down too far, I could manage a large amount of weight without problems.

And then my foot slipped!

When I lost control, the weight started pressing me into the steel plate at the bottom. I knew that if I tried to stop the descending weight with my knees, I'd blow out my joints. Unfortunately, I didn't realize that my ankles were just as vulnerable. With a horrible surge of torment, I watched my ankles start turning under. I could feel the muscles and tendons being pulled beyond their limits. A crunching sound echoed through my body and significant damage was done.

The weight smashed me down into a tight ball, knocking all the wind out of me. Quickly, I realized that I was in such a locked position that I could not breathe and started passing out. Voices echoed behind me as other members of the health club rushed to get the weights off. I could hear them shouting that they couldn't lift the hundred-pound weights off the machine.

"Out of the way!" Bill Cole's voice cut through the confusion. "This man is really injured."

I could hear the sound of the large iron plates being jerked off. When the iron bar was pushed up, I tumbled off the machine onto the floor.

"Get an ambulance!" Bill Cole shouted. "I think he's broken his back."

"No," I mumbled. "Just help me get to my feet."

"You can't get up," Cole protested. "Stay down."

"Help me stand up," I extended my hand. "I've got to go."

Bill Cole reluctantly got me up and helped me to my car. I drove home and started piling ice on my feet. Barely able to hobble around, I could see the swelling was expanding fast. When my wife walked into the kitchen, she stared in horror. With no other alternative but to show up for the wedding, I told her to call the church and have them put a chair in the middle of the chancel where I could sit down. No matter how badly I felt, I couldn't let the bride down.

Somehow, I got through the service and my wife whisked me off to the hospital. Only in the emergency room did I fully realize that I had cracked a couple of ribs. The agony from breathing quickly became worse than the broken ankles. By eleven o'clock that night, the attendants rolled me out in a wheelchair and I went home with a plaster cast on one leg and a plastic splint on the other because it was too swollen for plaster. A week later I was to return for a more durable device. I looked like a diesel truck had run over me!

During the week that followed, I had to be pushed around the church in a wheelchair. I wasn't about to let a little accident slow me down (which proved to be an extremely foolish idea). As the week wore on, the pain didn't decrease. In fact, my breathing became so difficult that I couldn't lie down in bed without my wife lowering me. The problems only seemed to increase in difficulty.

On Friday morning I was sitting in my office wrapped in so much excruciating discomfort that I didn't think I could stand it. Everything inside me cried, *Go home!* Agonizing over what to do, I tried to pray. During the week I had attempted to pray but didn't get anywhere because I hurt too much. This morning felt even worse and I only fumbled as I cried out for help.

I am going to touch your body, the voice seemed to say in my mind, and I thought Jesus Christ was speaking.

I stopped and opened my eyes. The startling pronouncement cut through my hurting, but that was all that happened. As the day unfolded, nothing followed and I concluded that I must have been talking to myself. However, by later afternoon I knew that I needed somebody to pray for me. My secretary called a few of the men that had been part of my training sessions on healing ministry to come on Saturday morning and intercede. I was hauled home with a thoroughly discouraged attitude.

The next morning eight men gathered around me and started praying. I wanted to pray with them, but every time I took a breath it hurt too much to more than mumble. One of the group began praying aloud and I tried to hang on. In the midst of his prayer I began to feel something unusual. At first I couldn't identify it, but slowly my feet began to tingle. It felt like the pain in my ankles was congealing, coming together, and starting to move up my legs like a cloud ascending.

The intercessors continued, but my attention was entirely fixed on the sensation of pain diminishing as it traveled up my body. I knew that my ankles no longer hurt and that was marvelous. I just didn't want the process to stop halfway.

"Oh Lord," the elder prayed, "by the power of Your resurrection, please raise Robert up and restore his ankles."

I could feel the pain raising up to my chest and I began to pray that the hand of God wouldn't stop working. The relief felt so good from what I had struggled with all week that I simply didn't want the work to stop. Suddenly, the haze of suffering lifted above my head and was gone. I sat there in astonishment. My body felt normal. All the hurting was gone!

The men kept praying, but even with my past experiences, I couldn't believe it. In a minute and a half the awful struggle was over. I interrupted their prayers and stood up.

"Look!" I shouted. "My ankles don't hurt!"

The men looked at me dumbfounded. They had

expected relief, but nothing of these proportions. I stood up and pushed the wheelchair back. Hobbling around with the casts on my feet, I went stumbling across the church to show my wife. Along the way I realized that my ribs no longer hurt. My gratitude overflowed like a flooding river!

Two weeks later I went back to the gym to work out again. I was unbuttoning my shirt in the locker room when Bill Cole walked by. Bill took a couple of steps and stopped. He turned around and looked at me like he was seeing a ghost.

"Wise?" Bill Cole said. "Aren't you Robert Wise? The guy we pulled off the hack squat machine?"

"Yeah," I said. "That's me."

"How can this be?" Bill said. "What are you doing in here exercising? I carried you to your car."

I asked him if he wanted the whole story because it was unusual, and Cole told me that he had all day to listen. I could tell by the look on his face that he was captivated.

"Maybe you don't believe in such things," I began, "but the Lord Jesus Christ healed me."

As Bill stood there with his mouth open, I related the entire event. Our church was located directly behind the gym and I invited him to attend. Bill kept shaking his head in amazement, but he assured me he would come to worship on Sunday.

Bill not only kept his word but attended the membership class. When Bill Cole joined the church I knew that he had encountered the living Christ and was going down the road on a new and special journey. Only later did it occur to me that Bill Cole had first helped me in my physical need and that opened the door for me to help him with his spiritual destination. The circle of unexpected grace had encompassed both of our lives.

As time went by, I saw that there was one other dimension to be remembered. When we give unexpectedly, we receive more than we could have imagined.

Sent Forth

RICK TORRENCE

Picture this: everything seems to have fallen into place. You've got a good job and so does your wife. Your children are doing well, and you're thinking that it's all coming together. Then you're told to give it up—everything you've worked for—and move.

That's the way it was for LaVerne and me in the fall of 1983. I was working construction for my dad, and LaVerne had been offered a tenure-track position at Syracuse University College of Nursing. We had three wonderful children—ages five, three, and one—and our parents lived close by. I was happy writing music for our church, where we were surrounded by family and good friends. To top it all off, our landlord had just told me how he liked the way we looked after the place. "Ricky," he said, "I'll make you a good deal for this house and the one next door."

Everything was going great for us.

Then, one winter night, as LaVerne and I were thanking God for all He had given us, we asked for His blessing to buy the houses. But God didn't give us the go-ahead or offer counsel about the mortgage or the new roof or any such thing. Instead, an inner voice came, saying, *If you desire to do my will, give away all that you possess and go to Peoria, Illinois, for I have a place for you there.*

Believe it or not, LaVerne and I both heard it and stared at each other. "Peoria?" I asked.

"Who do we know in Peoria?"

But then we prayed together again, and the answer came through clear as a bell: *If you truly want to be my servants, you will give away everything. I have a place for you in Peoria.*

Try explaining that to your mother-in-law. Try giving away all of your possessions—your furniture, your wedding presents and books, your wife's green Crock-Pot, your pickup and Mercury Marquis. Try meeting your friends' eyes as you tell them. Imagine having your wife leave a good job with full benefits. Imagine uprooting your children, resigning from your church duties.

Finally I had to tell my dad—this stern, hard-working, fifty-six-year-old man who had provided for fifteen children and who now counted on me as his right-hand man. I sat in his truck and told him I was leaving the company he'd struggled to build from scratch. "If God is telling you you gotta go," he said to me, staring straight out the windshield, "then you've gotta go, I guess."

If you can picture any shred of this—how unusual

and crazy we knew this must have sounded to the rest of the world—then you can glimpse some of what we went through as we packed a van with some clothes and our kids. We took four hundred dollars with us and headed west toward Illinois, leaving our home, our family, our lives in Syracuse behind.

It wasn't easy, but we knew we had to go. And as the highway opened up before us, we sang hours' worth of songs, which helped us endure the endless hum of the tires, the jostling of tractor-trailers, and the exits passing. I don't know quite what I expected when we reached Peoria.

Just over the town line, I pulled onto the side of the road. We had nowhere to go, really, so we sat and prayed. "We made this trip for you, Lord. Now where do we go?"

As it grew dark, LaVerne finally said, "Rick, let's find a motel. It's cold and the kids and I are shivering."

I eased us back onto the blacktop and pulled in at the first budget motel we saw. We waited there for the next three days, praying for direction. Still no response, but I reminded myself how God promised in the Bible, "I will never leave you nor forsake you." On Saturday, we paid for our final night in the motel, then ate dinner and counted out our last twelve dollars on the dresser. We didn't have enough money for another day, and we tucked the kids into bed knowing that we would have to sleep in the van the next night. As I paced the motel room and glanced at my sleeping children, a cold sweat ran down my back. Had I misunderstood God's will? Had I misled my family?

In the quite of the night, LaVerne and I got down on our knees again and prayed more fervently than ever. "Lord, thank You for watching over us," we said. "Thank You for bringing us this far. But where do we go now? What next, Lord?"

Out of the darkness, God spoke to us again. *Go to the Christian Assembly Church. Tell them I sent you, and they will give you everything you need.*

LaVerne and I looked at each other in disbelief. I grabbed the *Yellow Pages* from the nightstand drawer and rifled through them. The Christian Assembly Church was only two blocks from the motel! The next morning we rose early and dressed quickly to check out.

"Where are we going?" the kids asked, climbing into the van.

"To church!" LaVerne said. "Let's hurry or we'll miss the service."

With the gas needle on empty, we found the church, parked the van, and walked through the tall wooden doors. Every person in every pew seemed to turn to us— a sea of faces staring at us, not one black face in the whole congregation. If LaVerne and the kids hadn't started down the aisle, I don't believe I would have taken a step further, my pride having kicked in. I could guess what they were thinking: *What are* they *doing here? Who are they—some family wanting a handout?*

The preacher nodded as we slipped into a pew, then began the service, inquiring if there were any people here for the first time. I stood. "My wife and I are here with our children," I said and sat again. When it came time for the offering, we placed our last twelve dollars in the collection plate. As the service ended, people began filing out of the church. I bowed my head. "Lord," I prayed, "I thought you said they would help us."

Again God spoke to me. *Go and tell him what I told you in the motel.*

I rushed up to the pastor, and he told me to give the secretary our address for the mailing list.

"Pastor," I said, "we have no address. The Lord told us to come here and you would give us a place to stay. We came from New York, where I supervised the music in our church."

The preacher stepped back slightly. Then he called to those around him. "This is the family we've been praying for," he said with a terrific smile. "The new family that will bless us with their music!"

He walked us around the corner to a three-bedroom house and handed us a set of keys. In a matter of days his congregation generously gave us all the household items we needed, even a green crock-pot like the one LaVerne left behind in Syracuse.

We spent the next two years in Peoria, striving to be

a light in a city that faced rising unemployment and increasing crime. God continued to lead us. LaVerne won a job teaching nursing, while I started a community garden and opened our house to those in need. We ministered in that church, grew close to the parish, and helped serve them. We had learned what it meant to trust in God, without any pride.

LaVerne and I still prayed every day, so that we'd stay on the right path. "Why are we here?" we asked. "What should we do? How may we serve You best?"

I want you to go home, said the Lord one day. It was time to go back to New York.

It was no easier to leave Peoria than it had been to drive away from Syracuse. We were sad to say good-bye to our new friends at Christian Assembly. But this move was different. This time we knew with an even deeper faith that we were on the right path, and that we were home wherever God sent us.

We returned to our families and our church. I resumed my music ministry and went back to work for my father and LaVerne got a good nursing job. The Lord led us to another house. I still try telling people what it's like to trust in God no matter what. And I'm not so surprised now when they seem to understand, as they did in Peoria.

Message Imprinted
on a Heart

KATE R. THOMAS

Glancing out at the unusually gloomy day I prayed, "Lord, please bring our children home safely." Falling temperatures, coupled with a mixture of rain and sleet, caused deep concern. Our two children were driving home from their respective colleges in old worn-out cars. I had sensed the excitement in their phone conversations the previous night. They were looking forward to coming home for Thanksgiving and a much-needed break from studies.

My day of substitute teaching in one of Louisville's inner city schools seemed to move slowly. The noise level climbed rapidly with each passing minute. I reminded myself that it's always difficult to keep order in classrooms during the days before a holiday. I could not seem to shake the feelings of uneasiness, and my search for peace continued. *Lord, please help the old cars hold together. Protect our children from other vehicles and the highways from icing over.*

Then, like a miracle, these words saturated my mind: "Peace I leave with you; my peace I give to you; not as the world gives do I give to you. Let not your hearts be troubled, neither let them be afraid" (John 14:27 RSV).

The peace that came into my heart that day was real. I felt it and treasured it. But it seemed only temporary. I couldn't keep my eyes off the worsening weather outside. *I must stay on task with these children* came the reoccurring thought that brought me back to reality.

Suddenly, little hyperactive Jacob bounded from his desk and came toward me. His dark eyes sparkled with joy as he jumped up and down in front of my desk. My first impulse was to send him back to his seat, but before I could say anything, he commanded, "Hold out your hands!"

I obeyed.

"Close your eyes!" came the second command. I obeyed again, but a bit more reluctantly this time. I felt a small piece of plastic in my hands. When the "little general" gave me permission to open my eyes, I saw that I was holding a red plastic heart. I thanked Jacob sincerely and gestured for him to return to his seat.

"Well, read it!" he said, and I felt that he wanted to add "dummy!"

Seeing nothing on the top side, I turned the little heart over quickly. I didn't want Jacob to have to instruct me again. There before my eyes were these words, "Let not your hearts be troubled, neither let them be afraid"

(John 14:27 RSV). I felt this promise engraved on Jacob's plastic heart sink into my very being. Peace. Blessed peace filled me to overflowing. Pulling Jacob close to me, I confessed, "Jacob, you will never know how much these words mean to me today."

Jacob's face beamed brightly as he skipped back to his seat. I didn't have the heart to tell him that we are to walk, not skip, in the school building.

Jacob's message from God's Word that I received on that gloomy day in November has lasted through the years. The comfort and staying power of Christ's promise just before He faced the cross was imprinted on my heart now. So many times I have called upon John 14:27.

I remember an assignment in Washington D.C. with a group of women from throughout the United States. We were sent by our churches to visit a community center in the crime-ridden area of that city. Our responsibility was to discuss with some welfare recipients the present welfare system. Our hotel personnel warned us that we would probably have to wait a good while for transportation, because cab drivers were not eager to go to that part of town. We would also have to wait for someone to bring us back to the hotel.

When we arrived at the community center, it was obvious that we were not welcome. A barrage of angry words greeted us and continued around the discussion table. Tension increased with each passing second. Threats were hurled at us. I asked myself, *Why in the world am I here anyway?* I wanted to believe that I was there to try to make a difference in the world, and let people know that the Church cares for all people. But in that moment nothing seemed to make sense.

Voices became louder. I looked at the angry faces of the local women and also at the frightened faces of those who came with me. *Lord,* I prayed, *help me to know what to do or say.* Then, as though the Holy Spirit put the words in my mind, I remembered, "Peace I leave with you; my peace I give to you; not as the world gives do I give to you. Let not your hearts be troubled, neither let them be afraid" (John 14:27 RSV).

Standing on trembling legs, I began to pour out my heart to these women. I kept my voice low so that they would have to lower their own if they heard me. When voices were calmer, I told them that we cared about their plight in life and about them personally. I told them that the churches that we represented care for them too. Then I said, "Most of all, God cares for you." Quoting John 14:27 with them, I watched as facial expressions changed. Voices became kind. Eyes no longer glared angrily at us.

An hour later the meeting concluded in a spirit of reconciliation. We walked to the street to wait for a taxi, but we were not alone. These local women stood outside with us for forty-five minutes while we waited for another brave cab driver. I believe that a miracle through the power of God's Word happened that day. The Bible promises that His word will not return to us void.

Years later my husband, daughter, and I were traveling by boat from the Netherlands to England. Images of the breathtaking beauty of Holland's tulips and daffodils brought smiles to our faces as the old ship moved slowly out into the English Channel. Little did we suspect that trouble was ahead.

Soon a fierce storm arose. The boat, which was headed for dry dock for repairs, creaked and groaned, rocking haphazardly to and fro. Chairs, tables, food items, drinks, and even people scrambled in every direction. Motion sickness medicine ran out. It was a scary time. And again, God's comforting Word brought the miracle of peace. *"Let not your heart be troubled, neither let it be afraid."* I repeated these words over and over. The world could never bring the kind of peace that I felt in that storm. God spared us, and we will be grateful forever.

Finally, today God reminded me again of the power in His Word. Tomorrow I face a heart procedure. I opened my devotional books for my morning quiet time, and what was before my eyes? "Peace I leave with you: my peace I give to you; not as the world gives, do I give to you. Let not your hearts be troubled, neither let them be afraid" (John 14:27 RSV). Was that a coincidence? I doubt it. Rather, I believe it was a God-incidence.

Lord, I am finally getting your message. You want to give us a miracle. Your peace, the kind of peace that the world cannot give. You don't want us to worry or be afraid. I can lay every need and concern before you, and know that you are sovereign. You are in control. You want the best for Your children. Thank you, Lord.

Jacob reminded me many years ago of God's promise of peace. The Scripture message imprinted on that little plastic heart became permanently imprinted on my own heart. By focusing on God's sufficiency and the promises in His Word, we can experience miracles in the midst of life's storms. Thanks be to God.

A Woman of Faith

CHARLES G. FINNEY

Brother Charles Finney was born in 1792. He was educated at Yale, and at age twenty-six he was admitted to the New York bar. On October 10, 1821, he experienced a dramatic religious conversion and set aside his practice to preach. He became the president of Oberlin College in 1851. Finney was a prolific writer until his death in 1875. The following unedited story is taken from his memoirs.

I found in Syracuse a Christian woman whom they called "Mother Austin," a woman of most remarkable faith. She was poor and entirely dependent upon the charity of the people for subsistence. She was an uneducated woman, and had been brought up manifestly in a family of very little cultivation. But she had such faith as to secure the confidence of all who knew her. The conviction seemed to be universal among both Christians and unbelievers, that Mother Austin was a saint. I do not think I ever witnessed greater faith in its simplicity than was manifested by that woman. A great many facts were related to me respecting her, that showed her trust in God, and in what a remarkable manner God provided for her wants from day to day.

She said to me on one occasion, "Finney, it is impossible for me to suffer for any of the necessaries of life, because God has said to me, 'Trust in the Lord and do good: so shalt thou dwell in the land, and verily thou shalt be fed.'" What a great message!

She related to me many facts in her history, and many facts were related to me by others, illustrative of the power of her faith.

She said one Saturday evening a friend of hers, but an impenitent man, called to see her; and after conversing awhile he offered her, as he went away, a five-dollar bill. She said that she felt an inward admonition not to take it. She felt that it would be an act of self-righteousness on the part of that man, and might do him more harm than it would do her good. She therefore declined to take it, and he went away. She said she had just wood and food enough in the house to last over the Sabbath, and that was all; and she had no means whatever of obtaining any more. But still she was not at all afraid to trust God, in such circumstances, as she had done for so many years.

On the Sabbath there came a violent snow-storm. On Monday morning the snow was several feet deep, and the streets were blocked up so that there was no getting out without clearing the way. She had a young son that lived with her, the two composing the whole family. They arose in the morning and found themselves snowed in, on every side. They made out to muster fuel enough for a little fire, and soon the boy began to inquire what they should have for breakfast.

She said, "I do not know, my son; but the Lord will provide." She looked out, and nobody could pass the streets. The lad began to weep bitterly, and concluded that they should freeze and starve to death. However, she said she went on and made such preparations as she could, to provide for breakfast, if any should come. I think she said she set her table, and made arrangements for her breakfast, believing that some would come in due season.

Very soon she heard a loud talking in the streets, and went to the window to see what it was, and beheld a man in a single sleigh, and some men with him shoveling the snow so that the horse could get through. Up they came to her door, and behold! they had brought her a plenty of fuel and provision, everything to make her comfortable for several days.

But time would fail me to tell the instances in which she was helped in an amazing manner as striking as this. Indeed, it was notorious through the city, so far as I could learn, that Mother Austin's faith was like a bank; and that she never suffered for want of the necessaries of life, because she drew on God.

CHAPTER 2

You've Got Mail!

Hold firmly to the trustworthy message as it has been taught, so you can encourage others. (Titus 1:9 NIV, adapted)

Letters. Telegrams. Packages. And yes, e-mail. Messages come in many different sizes, shapes, and formats, whether in your postal box or through cyberspace. Mail brings us messages of hope and joy. It connects us with our families and friends. It lets us know we are part of a world community held together by the wonder of words.

A Miracle of Song

ELIZABETH SCHMEIDLER

Saturday morning—normally a day to sleep in a bit, but since I was scheduled to sing a special Mass on Monday, I wanted to rehearse and organize my music. The thought gave me great pleasure, so I threw the covers aside and sprang out of bed.

As I made my way to the bathroom, I cleared my voice—something that had become a regular habit for me. As a singer, having a clear voice was obviously essential. For me, it was more than that—a clear voice was a miracle.

I was thirty-six years old when our church organist walked up to me and asked me to consider singing for Mass. It would have been easier if he had asked me to take a flying leap to the moon. I had never sung solo in my whole life—in fact, except for at Mass, I kept my singing to myself. I figured that I must be one of those people who think they sound sort of good in the shower but are really bad singers . . . surely someone would have told me otherwise. Yet, in the past months, people had been turning around after Mass and telling me that

I should be singing up front. It was a strange and very frightening prospect to me—one, because this had never happened before, but suddenly was happening on a regular basis, and two, because I was the type of person who couldn't say their names at a baby shower without breaking into a sweat!

To make a long story short, I was scared to death and worried I would fail, but I knew that God was up to something, so I decided to pray for courage and read scriptures to strengthen me. Finally, with my knees knocking and my stomach churning, I sang solo in front of a full congregation. I began to feel God's peace come over me, and I knew I was experiencing a miracle. Only God could have given me the voice and the courage to serve Him this way, and I wanted to praise His name forever with my voice and my life.

But every fairytale has a conflict, and my fairytale is no different—I began experiencing long bouts of hoarseness. This was puzzling because I would wake up hoarse without any other symptoms. My voice would just be gone. As frustrating as this was, I was determined to keep singing. I babied my voice, drank water and any other medicinal concoction I could find, and oh, how I prayed! Occasionally, I would be hoarse the week before I was scheduled to sing at a wedding, and yet somehow, by God's grace, it would clear just in time. Still, I couldn't deny that the hoarseness was getting worse, and happening more frequently. With the Mass just two days away, I was apprehensive.

As I stepped into the shower and cleared my throat repeatedly, I finally had to face what I somehow already sensed—my voice was gone. *No . . . not again . . . please, Lord.* I leaned my head back and let the hot water pour over my throat, but I knew, deep down, that the problem was much worse than a hot shower could fix. Soon, my tears ran as quickly as the water down the shower doors.

Afterward, I drank some hot tea and tried to tell myself to have faith and that it would get better; but contrary to my attempts to think positive, my voice actually got worse throughout the day. By late afternoon I was trying to make up my mind about whether to call in another singer. Maybe it was selfish, but I had helped pick out the music, rehearsed it over and over so I would give God my very best, and I just didn't want to give up. Tears began to flow again as I fell to my knees. *Oh God . . . why? Why me? I have tried so hard to serve You. Why would You help me to sing and then take my voice away?*

I was sobbing by now and began to feel a bit of shame with each self-absorbed word I prayed, yet I couldn't stop. I was well aware that God already knew my thoughts and intentions, and somehow I sensed He understood and would forgive my sorrow. Sure enough, within moments I began to feel more peaceful. I asked God for a word from Him that would give me an answer—or at least help me accept what I couldn't understand. I let my Bible fall open to where it would, and my tears formed a lens of sort that magnified Psalm 40. The words I read made me cry even harder, because I knew that at that moment in time, they were for me. Not only was God assuring me that He heard my cry, He was also acknowledging my efforts to continually praise Him by giving Him all the credit for any courage and talents I possessed. In addition, the psalm helped me to realize that God knew how painful it was for me to know that there were people who claimed that my motivation for singing was to "show off." Only God completely understood why I sang with such passion—He had set me free. His opinion will always be the only One that matters.

At that moment I experienced God's powerful presence and felt led to sit down at the piano. God's blessing flowed through my mind and fingers as I composed (another miracle brought about by God) the melody and words to a song I entitled "Why Me?"

Psalm 40 spoke of putting a new song into my mouth, and indeed, He did! This gave me renewed confidence that despite the current circumstances, my voice would be back for the Mass. And it was! Just one day later, I sang nine songs, including four prelude solos. It was a miracle. I will never forget that Mass as long as I live.

In the months following, it was discovered that the hoarseness I was experiencing was caused by acid from

my stomach that had been washing back up my esopha-
gus, and creating ulcers on my vocal fold. Surgery was
needed to repair this. This time, when I was being
wheeled into the operating room, I didn't say, "Why
me?" but rather I thanked God for the gift of eternal life
that He has made possible no matter what comes our
way. I surrendered my life into His hands and He did not
let me down. Though I have not recorded the song yet,
I know that someday God will have me use it as He sees
fit. He does, indeed, care about all things, both great and
small.

Don't Ask My Wife to Pray for You!

NORRIS BURKES

U nless you're really serious, I wouldn't suggest that you ask my wife to pray for you. Trust me. This girl's got a reputation for knowing the meaning of the verse that says, "I will do whatever you ask in my name, so that the Son may bring glory to the Father. You may ask me for anything in my name, and I will do it" (John 14:13–14 NIV).

Her reputation is that if she prays for you, it might hurt.

A few years back she decided to pray for Sara, our college-student daughter who was so heavily involved in college busyness that we could rarely get her to answer her cell phone. My wife's prayer was that Sara would find a way to get more rest.

A week later, Sara broke her thumb and had to drop several extracurricular activities.

Apparently the prayer was a doozy, because this

wasn't your everyday broken thumb. It was a break that required her to fly home from school, find a specialist, and have surgery.

About that same time, Becky prayed to find more quality time to spend with our twelve-year-old daughter, Nicole. The day after Sara returned to school having recovered from thumb surgery, Nicole broke her foot. The doctor prescribed no walking, and Nicole spent many hours with my wife over the next two months. Prayer granted.

Then Becky turned her prayers loose on me. Like Sara, I, too, had been keeping a hectic schedule, and Becky prayed that I'd slow my writing schedule so I could spend more quality time with my family. Her prayer locked on to me sometime Saturday afternoon as I finished one writing project and was assembling my entry for a writing contest while also working on a sermon I had promised to preach for our pastor and making cross-country travel arrangements to receive an award I had won.

Suddenly, in the midst of all this multitasking, I grabbed my chest. It hurt to breathe, and the pain stretched from my navel to my throat. I wanted to think heartburn and feel confident I'd be okay, but as a hospital chaplain, I've heard too many people sing the heartburn tune of denial only to have it quickly become their funeral dirge. So with the calm demeanor of a drowning rat, I asked Becky to take me to the emergency room. Within a few minutes of my arrival, I was given my first nitroglycerin tablet.

Nitro tablets are what the ER staff gives middle-aged men who are suffering angst about their health. It gives you a nice headache, which helps you forget about your chest pain. Well, the short version of this story is that I stayed twenty-three hours for observation and was released the following day.

Diagnosis: heartburn

Person to blame (at least in my opinion): my loving wife and her prayers.

Lesson learned: when you're married to a prayer warrior, you *will* end up doing the right thing, one way or the other!

Becky's prayer hit its mark with accurate precision; it hadn't been intended as a fatal blow to my extracurricular writing activities. It was merely a warning shot over my bow, or perhaps more accurately, it was intended only to wing me. That's exactly what happened. My busy schedule slowed significantly, and Becky put another notch in her prayer belt.

But I want you to know that I, too, know the meaning of another powerful verse on prayer. My experience with the verse goes back to a junior high boys' camp where my camp counselor shared his secret for finding the most wonderfully caring and stunningly gorgeous woman in the world. Of course, all we cared about back then were the stunning-and-gorgeous parts, but we listened anyway as he opened his Bible and read a passage from Matthew: "Seek first [God's] kingdom and his righteousness, and all these things will be given to you as well" (6:33).

We stared at him blankly. Then one of my tent mates expelled an unbelieving grunt, prompting the counselor to explain: "If you follow that advice," he said, "it won't matter what the woman looks like to anyone else. To you, she'll be stunningly gorgeous."

With that anticlimactic remark, he slammed shut his Bible and turned off the light.

His words had an unexpected effect on me. As I lay there looking up at the ceiling of our tent, I was suddenly certain of two things: I wanted to be a minister, and I wanted a really fine girl. (And like most boys my age, the majority of my attention was on the latter.) Those are the things I prayed for that night . . . and for many nights after.

Despite my typically skewed adolescent priorities, ten years later God gave me "a really fine girl." Knowing what I know now, I'm sure our meeting came about more as result of her prayers than from my own prayerful requests that began with the testosterone-charged plea that night at camp. Now, after twenty-eight years of marriage, she continues to pray for me, continually asking

God to help me keep my priorities straight by seeking his will for my life.

Her prayers sometimes take a circuitous route, and yes, sometimes people have been slightly injured in the process, but everyone's okay in the end. So lately I've been thinking of posting a prayer-request list on my Web site, offering to ask Becky to pray for those who sign up. But I warn you: don't ask her unless you're serious. And don't be surprised if I ask you to sign a release form first!

The Envelope

KATHRYN LAY

My dream of motherhood seemed to be disappearing, our longed-for child had not arrived. After the tenth negative pregnancy test in less than five years, I had given up hope of ever being called Mama.

"Why?" I continually asked God. We weren't asking for anything wrong. We wanted to be parents. We wanted children to love and raise and teach, children to share God's love with and to see lead happy lives. I couldn't understand why we were being punished, why this prayer was going unanswered.

My husband and I were surrounded by pregnant family and friends, by new nieces and nephews. We loved them all, but it was a constant reminder of the loss we were feeling. Every time another friend or family member announced they would be having a baby, a second baby, even a third, I felt I had died inside all over again.

Our friends tried to be a comfort, tried to say the things that would ease our hurt. But somehow, the words pushed us into feelings of guilt. Had we angered God that this prayer wasn't being answered? Were we just meant to be childless? There were even those who suggested that we had done something wrong, disobeyed God somehow, so He was punishing us in this way. I knew deep down this wasn't true, but at times, I wondered.

"Don't you love us anymore?" I asked God one morning. "I don't understand why I'm not pregnant yet."

Later that week, a dear friend came by my house, holding her newborn son. I held him in my arms and wondered what it would be like to hold my own child. My heart broke, but I tried to keep a smile for my friend.

"Kathy, I can't help but see you as a mother someday. I see God working in this in an amazing way."

I burst into tears, wanting to believe her but afraid of holding on to my dream and finding only disappointment. It seemed that after so long there was no more hope in my heart. Could Richard and I live our lives childless, grandchildless? Could we find other things to occupy us, obsess over a dog or our careers instead?

"What will your first child's name be?" she asked.

"Michael or Michelle," I answered. Richard and I had long chosen these names, meaning "strength of God," even before we married. Every time a friend had a baby, I wondered when one would name their child the same.

Darla wrote something on a piece of paper, folded it, and asked me for an envelope. She put the paper inside and sealed it. "Open this when he or she arrives."

I put the envelope in a pocket of my purse, figuring I would never have the opportunity to read what was inside.

"Have faith," she said before she left.

I really wanted to; I wanted to trust God in this, but it wasn't easy. I could only keep praying for that miracle.

Five years went by. Richard and I still longed for a child, but put our efforts into careers and ministry work. I sold all the baby items I'd been buying at garage sales over the years. It was just too painful to be reminded of our lost dream.

At one point I went through a false pregnancy, and we had begun putting together a nursery. I gave away all the furniture and turned the room into an office.

Then one morning a friend who had also tried for many years to have a child called to tell us about the classes she and her husband were taking to be eligible for adoption through the state. We signed up right away.

Could we hope again? Was this God's design for our prayers for a child, through adoption?

Seven months later, we'd been approved to be adoptive parents. Our classes and home studies were done. Hours of weekly classes, stacks of paperwork, dozens of visits to our home, physicals and interviews were finally completed.

It was time to wait.

Again I waited, as I'd done before. But this time, the

hope was stronger. And on November 2, 1992, the call came. We had been accepted for a nine-month-old girl.

The moment I saw my daughter crawling toward us, our dreams for parenthood came true. She wasn't born to us physically, but in hopes and prayers and long years of dreaming, she would soon be our daughter for life.

Her foster parents had named her Michelle.

When I was told her name, I knew only God had brought this all together so perfectly. She was even the image of my husband and still, fifteen years later, people comment on how much alike they look.

It wasn't until nearly a year after she came into our lives, cleaning out my closet that I found an old purse. I rummaged through it as my daughter played around my feet. In a zippered pocket was an envelope.

I opened it and read the note my friend had written.

Kathy, give little Michael or Michelle a hug for me. Never give up faith or hope.

I glanced down at Michelle and smiled. She grinned back. "Play, Mama."

My friend had planted seeds of faith in my heart. God had watered them, and my dream came to life and called me Mama.

The Quilting Cure

JUDY TIPTON RUSH

Strokes don't hurt. At least, mine didn't. I woke up one bright June morning in 1999 to the sound of the radio and the smell of the bacon my husband, Ed, was frying in the kitchen. I felt a little groggy, but not much worse than I usually do before my first cup of coffee. I threw off the big warm handmade quilt, pulled on my robe, and went downstairs. Just as I stepped into the kitchen, the phone rang. I grabbed it before Ed could answer.

"Hello?" I said, trying to sound cheerful. But something else came out. *Was that my voice?* The word sounded strange, garbled. Maybe I was still dreaming.

"Judy?" the person on the other end asked, apparently as confused as I was. "Is that you?" I opened my mouth to answer. I couldn't. I turned to Ed, trying to call for help. Like in a nightmare, my lips moved, but no words came out.

Ed rushed me to the hospital. I collapsed in the emergency room.

I hadn't been dreaming, the doctor informed me. I'd had a stroke, and there would be some damage.

"It could've been much worse," the doctor tried to reassure me. "Because Ed got you here so quickly, you have a good chance of recovering. It'll take time and physical therapy, but you should consider yourself lucky. Very lucky."

Lucky? I thought. *Right.*

I was the self-sufficient, independent type, the girl who could type sixty-five words a minute without making a single mistake and crack a joke or tell a story with the best of them. Our house was decorated with my watercolors. My hand-sewn quilts had won prizes and had been exhibited at shows around the world.

Inside, I felt the same as ever, raring to go. But outside—what a difference! I'd lost all power of speech. I couldn't use my right arm or my right leg at all. Yes, physical therapy was my best hope. But my progress was slow. I had to learn to walk again, step by step, like a toddler. I had to learn to speak again, using word association to remember even simple words. If I forgot the word *apple*, for instance, I'd repeat *fruit, round, color, red* over and over until it stuck in my mind.

At six months my right foot continued to drag like a ball and chain. I constantly had to stop mid-sentence to grope for words. It was maddening. After a year of therapy, I couldn't even grocery shop on my own. It was still a struggle to do things like dial a phone number or send an e-mail. Never mind quilting.

"Judy, you're not going to get better overnight," Ed reminded me. "You have to be patient."

I knew that recovery took time. It was just that I expected to have made more progress by this point. *I've been working so hard in therapy, Lord, I have been patient, haven't I?*

My physical therapist recommended needlework to improve my fine motor skills. Why not give cross-stitch a try? I loved sewing and quilting. Still, Ed had to thread the needle for me. That was annoying. Then I couldn't get the darn thing to do what I wanted. I ended up with a mess of chaotic lines. I pricked my fingers so many times I felt like a pincushion. I threw the square in the trash.

One day my friend Sharon dropped by. "How's the needlework going?" she asked. Sharon and I belonged to the same quilt guild. A lot of my friends were members, and I really missed our meetings. Not just the quilting, but all the gabbing.

"Just fine," I said, tight-lipped.

"Maybe you can start quilting again," she went on. "I'm using one of those computerized sewing machines now. It's amazing! They perform so much better than the old ones. You should see. There's going to be a quilt festival in Houston in a few months. Why don't you come along with me?"

I stole a glance at my useless hands. "Maybe," I told Sharon. "But I don't think so."

I couldn't get Sharon's invitation to the quilt festival out of my head. But I had to admit, the thought of going all the way to Houston scared me. I still had trouble telling my left from my right. How could I make my way through an airport or navigate a strange city? It would be nice to see those quilts, though . . .

I told Ed what was on my mind.

"You should go," he urged me. "No question about it."

"But I don't even know if I'll ever be able to quilt again."

"You'll never know if you don't try," he replied.

The next time Sharon stopped by, I got up my courage and said I'd go.

I was a little worried about the plane trip to Houston. How would I be able to keep up a conversation, even with a good friend, for that long? My words came haltingly, but the more Sharon and I joked and talked, the easier it seemed to be for me to communicate. Before I knew it, we were landing in Houston.

"Chatting with you is some kind of speech therapy," I told Sharon.

At the festival, every wall was decorated with unbelievable quilts. Designs so intricate I hadn't known that you could make them with a machine. At least, not with any machine I'd ever had. I just stared at them. Each quilt was more amazing than the last.

"These are stunning," I said to Sharon. "Think of how much time it must take to make one of them."

"And how much patience," she said.

That word. Suddenly, I saw those quilts in a different light. They hadn't come together in a moment. Someone had worked at them, day by day, step by step, stitch by stitch. The way God was working on me, a little at a time. The message couldn't have been clearer: just look at what you can do with a little patience. *Thank you, Lord, for being patient with me.*

Soon as I got home, I told Ed all about the quilts at the festival.

"You know what, Judy?" he said. "You need to get one of those computerized sewing machines."

"We can swing it," Ed insisted. "I haven't seen you this excited about something in ages. You just talked for fifteen minutes without once pausing for a word. I think quilting would do you a world of good."

We went to Memphis a few days later and picked up a new computerized sewing machine. That evening I set to work. I decided to start with a cat pattern I'd designed myself. The moment I turned on the machine and guided the fabric through, I felt the difference. It was smoother, more precise. Even with my shaky hands, it was easy to follow patterns. I worked on the quilt late into the night. I was back at it first thing the next morning. When I finally finished that first quilt, I stretched it out on the floor in the living room. Then I called Ed in.

"What do you think?" I asked excitedly. He stared at it for a few minutes.

"I think it's just as good as anything you did before the stroke," he said. Then he smiled. "In fact, I think it's even better."

Since then, I have made dozens of quilts—all sorts of patterns, from flowers to moons and stars. Sharon and I have joined a new quilting group we call the Knot Crazies. We meet once a month. The talking plays as much a part in my recovery as the quilting. I can speak clearly now and do everyday tasks on my own.

The big things, like quilting—and healing—take more. More help. More time. More patience. But believe me, they're worth the wait.

One Single Leaf

JAN COREY ARNETT

When my father's cancer was diagnosed, he and my mother decided to move near me and take advantage of medical care that was not readily available in their rural community. I was their youngest daughter, and honored to be able to help them. But Dad had another reason. My husband and I have a few acres where we keep cattle and horses, a garden and some woods. Dad, I knew, had given some consideration to that.

For years Mom and Dad had worked their farm in Michigan's Upper Peninsula. My father loved the land and the woods. He cut his own firewood and fence posts and made a few dollars from the sale of timber. Mostly, though, the woods were his spiritual retreat. Dad said he often felt even closer to God while resting on a mossy stump watching deer and squirrels than he did while sitting in a pew on Sunday.

Every season held something wondrous for Dad. He loved the wildflowers of spring and the fragrance of evergreens after a summer rain. Every fall he and Mom made a "color tour" around the state. Even the hushed solitude of the woods in the winter brought joy to Dad.

After they moved near us in Battle Creek, he and Mom drove over to our place to enjoy the feel of the country. While Mom picked wild blueberries, Dad dreamed aloud of clearing the underbrush from our woods. But his declining health never permitted him to do more than dream, and Dad was not able to go for the long walks that had given him such spiritual regeneration through the years.

One bright blue day late last October, Mom and I took Dad for an appointment at the oncology unit of the local medical center. Afterward, Dad tried to be cheerful—even though the cancer was advancing rapidly. I patted his shoulder as I wheeled him toward the car, feeling profoundly sad. Suddenly, in the middle of that large, treeless, windless parking lot, a single perfect maple leaf drifted dreamily down from above, landing in front of Dad's wheelchair, settling at his feet. Dad leaned over, picked it up, and smiled.

Not long after, Dad left the maple trees and his beloved woods behind. I still have that maple leaf on my desk. It reminds me that when my father was too weak to go to the woods, God brought the woods to him.

Through Tiny Windows

LISA JOHNSON

Michael always sat on the outer edge of the semi-circle—our classroom equivalent of the back row. He was two years older than the rest of the students, adopted from Mexico, and wore hearing aids in each ear. And Alison, his sign language interpreter, was always with him. Otherwise, Michael was nearly invisible for the first few months of the school year, and all my attempts to get him to mingle with the other students had failed.

As part of an awareness program, I decided to show my English class *Children of a Lesser God*, the break-through movie for deaf actress Marlee Matlin. I convinced Michael to help me with the lesson, so he moved his seat to the front of the room. The other students drifted in, noting Michael's change of seats, but like shy birds, they stayed quiet. They glanced at me for a clue, but I said nothing to ease their curiosity and simply started the movie.

When the lights came back on, Michael fidgeted, mostly rubbing the hairs of his new goatee. Otherwise there was silence.

Finally, Brenda, a dark-haired girl, spoke to Michael from across the room: "Do people tease you ever?" It was the first time one of them had addressed him directly, and I was, at first, afraid.

"Yes. All the time in middle school." Picking at the skin around his cuticles, he glanced back down. "But I've grown out of it now."

"That's so wrong," someone else offered. The wall clock hummed. Everyone but Michael could hear the words of the teacher next door lecturing on *The Catcher in the Rye* as our room fell silent again.

Michael scraped the corner of his desk with a pen. I remained in my chair, holding back an urge to take over and fill the silence with my own words. A few more seconds passed. Then Steven, a shy kid two desks down from the window, cleared his throat.

"What's your favorite sign?"

Michael shrugged. Everyone waited.

"I'll tell you mine," Alison answered, relieving us all. "Captivating." Her eyes widened as her fingers wiffled through the air, meeting in the center of her body.

Michael ran his fingers over the left side of his face, pushing at the soft spots of skin between the new little bristles. "I know," he said, making a decision. "Touch the way." His hands fluttered, caterpillarlike, one arm hovering half a second above the other, before he yanked them back, crossing them against his chest.

"Do it again," his classmates urged. It was the first time we'd seen him sign. He usually just read lips, studied the overhead notes in the dark, and tried to vocalize when called on in class. It was as though his deafness was a shameful secret. In repetition, the movements became as graceful as a song, which they may have been.

The class watched with fascination, as if charmed by an urban serpent. "How many signs do you know?"

"Can you play sports if you can't hear?"

"Wait a minute—if only your mom knows sign language, how do you communicate with your dad and sister?"

They were asking so fast he couldn't answer. He smiled. They were paying attention. He was finally important.

"Why don't you have your driver's license?"

"If you were born deaf, why did it take so long for anyone to notice?"

"Sign your name." He did.

This was better than any activity I could have planned. We had already walked around the hallways wearing blindfolds, drawn trees with pens in our mouths, and tried to peek through some tiny window into what it felt like to be handicapped, if only for a few moments. But none of those activities compared to the lesson that Michael was giving us now.

In the back of room 211E, the rear wall reflected the sun's pale glare onto the faces of the students who were sometimes interested, often bored. These same students were now clambering beneath Michael's surface in ways the rest of us could never do. We would have been too afraid, too tactful.

A buzz began in my classroom that morning and rose joyfully to the fluorescent bulbs above us.

"Could I learn sign language?" someone asked.

"Yeah! That would be so cool." A chorus of students chimed in. A smile, real this time, began to glisten at the edge of Michael's face. He slapped his hands melodically against the bars of his chair, leaning back so that its legs lifted off the floor.

How do you thank someone for noticing a person who really needs to be seen? That day, I did not know how to express my intense gratitude to those students. I could only stammer good-bye at the end of class.

A Book and a Bond

LISA ALLRED

L isa, I need to talk to you," said Debbie, walking toward me from across the room. We were standing in the classroom where we both attend a Bible Study Fellowship (BSF) meeting each week. BSF is a nondenominational Bible study, so women from many different churches meet together.

Debbie recently lost her twenty-seven-year-old son, Joshua, in an industrial accident. And she has obviously been distressed over her loss. So the week before, I had brought Debbie a copy of a book entitled *Little Taps on the Shoulder from God*, which my friend had written and which contains the story of the death of my three-year-old son, Robby, in a drowning accident twenty-four years ago. I thought it might comfort her in some small way and help us to connect.

Robby had been riding his little tricycle around his grandmother's swimming pool while she and her brother-in-law were cleaning out the pool shed. When she realized she hadn't heard Robby for a few minutes, she stepped out of the shed to see where he was and discovered him face down in the pool. He died about four days later in a local hospital, leaving me devastated, just as Debbie was now.

"Sure, Debbie. How can I help?" I asked.

"I wanted to say thank you for the book you gave me last week. It was very helpful."

"Good. I'm glad it helped."

"I was especially struck by the story about your Robby. I guess we have a lot in common."

"Yes, unfortunately, I guess we do."

"Tell me, Lisa," she went on with a little more intensity, "before Robby died, did he attend a daycare center in Hurst?"

Thinking back, I said, "Why, yes, he did. But how did you know that?" This news came as a surprise to me.

"Because one of my son's best friends drowned about that time while they were attending the same daycare. What was the name of the daycare where Robby attended?"

"Let's see," I said, trying to remember. "Was it Horton's? Or maybe Harper's?"

"Could it have been Harberts?" she asked tentatively.

"Yes, that's it—Harberts. And that's where your son went too?"

"Yes. In fact, I'm pretty sure Robby and Joshua were best friends," she said with a slight smile.

"Really?" I was still a bit shocked by her news.

"Yes. I don't know if you remember or not, but the minister at Robby's funeral talked about Robby's best friend, Joshua, and how they had been such great pals."

"Well, yes, now that you mention it, I do remember that. And Joshua was your son?" I asked incredulously.

"Yes. Can you believe it?" she said with a touch of melancholy. "Some coincidence, huh?"

Suddenly we had an instant bond, and I hugged her as our individual memories of little Robby and her Joshua held us together for a moment. Then we discovered that we also attend the same large church, but we don't run into each other because we go to different services.

Coincidence? I don't think so. The message of God's love in a special book formed a bridge and created a bond that will, no doubt, last a lifetime.

The Night Francine Left for College

GILLIAN EDOZIEN

A re you going to call your daughter?" I asked, standing in the doorway of the garage as my husband sanded the old rocking chair.

"You just talked to her an hour ago," he said without looking up.

"I know I talked to her. I asked if *you* were going to call her."

"Why would I call her?" He continued to rub away the dark stain of the wood.

"Aren't you curious?" I asked him. I felt like crying.

"Francine left yesterday. You talked to her a few hours ago, and she's fine." He looked up at me. "Stop worrying about her, okay? She'll be fine. So will you."

I had been in labor for barely an hour when Francine was born. Gary and I argued on the way to the hospital. Instead of putting both hands on the steering wheel, he insisted on trying to wipe my forehead with a damp cloth. It was the middle of August, and we were living in

southern Georgia at the time, so the heat was unbear-
able. He was kind to want to make me more comfortable, but as he nervously tried to swipe the damp
washcloth across my brow, he ran over three curbs while
turning corners. The violent jolt of the car hitting the
curb made me shriek, and I felt like I couldn't hold on to
the baby any longer.

When we entered the hospital, I was asked if I
needed a wheelchair. I said, "As long as you're driving
and he's not, that'll be fine."

Gary burst into tears. His body-jerking cries scared
me and the nurse who wheeled me down the hall. He
sobbed uncontrollably, saying over and over, "I'm just so
happy. I'm just so happy." One minute after arriving in
the delivery room, with Gary still sniffling, without doctors but with a more-than-competent nurse, our baby
daughter was born.

A little shy of eighteen years later, Gary sat calmly
with me at the kitchen table and lectured me about letting go. "This will be a wonderful move for her," he said
quietly.

"I know," I responded.

"This is such an exciting time for her. You should be
happy."

"I know. I am."

I know. I know. I know.

Francine was an early walker, an early talker, and

thankfully, an early riser. She inherited that from me. We're both light sleepers and usually out of bed by 6:00 A.M. During the past few years, I would often come downstairs in the morning to find Francine sitting at the table, drinking tea and listening to the radio. We would sit together and talk. Usually, we'd talk about seemingly inconsequential things, but I came to see it as an important time for us. They say that parents need to spend more time with their children to guide them and be aware of what they're up to. I agree, but I also wanted to spend time with Francine because I enjoyed her. It's as simple as that.

"Do you think she's making friends?" I asked my husband later that night while he was brushing his teeth in preparation for bed. "She's kind of shy. I wonder if I caused that. Did I let her be too clingy when she was little?" I took advantage of Gary's temporary inability to speak. "I wonder if she's prepared. If she's extending herself to people. She's quiet, and I wonder if she'll be overlooked by people."

Gary had heard enough. "Stop it, please! You and I both know that she's fabulous with people. I'm sure she's fine. I'm very confident about Fran. Why would you say she's shy? Come on, let's go to bed. Stop worrying. You'll call her tomorrow."

Stop worrying, he says. When does a mother get to stop worrying?

Gary fell asleep, and I lay in bed, wondering where Francine was at that minute. Is she lying awake, retracing her day? Is she trying to remember the names of the people she's met in her dorm? Is she thinking about her first day of classes tomorrow—will she find the building on time, does she have all her books? Is she not sleeping? Has this newfound freedom taken over my sensible daughter—will she be careful? Will she get in strange cars? Will she begin drinking? Will she make sensible friends? Will she remember everything that we tried to teach her, or will she forget? Did we miss anything important? Will she remember to pray?

I carefully got out of bed so as not to disturb Gary. In the dark, I reached for the radio on the kitchen counter and listened to Fran's favorite station. In the darkness, I tried to see her face, her eyes, the way she gently pulls her hair off her face. And in the darkness, I wondered if I'd ever recover from this, if it was completely unnatural to feel such loss as my daughter embarked on such an important journey. I wondered if my worrying would affect her poorly. I wanted to be able to take an appropriate step back, so that our relationship could transform. I wanted to see her whole, even if that meant she had to be away from me. I wanted to enjoy the woman that she had become.

How does it come so easily for Gary? I wondered. *Fran is his only child. Is it possible that a father just doesn't hold on as long or as hard? Would I want that? Should I work toward that?*

Francine went to her senior prom with a boy whom I'd met a few times. His name was Thomas, and Francine worked feverishly to make sure everything about their big night was perfect. When the doorbell rang, Francine walked into the living room wearing a long, sleeveless, boat-necked navy dress. My husband eyed Thomas suspiciously, but kept his words to a minimum. Francine came home on time, happy and satisfied with her prom experience. Her father pretended to casually get out of bed to see how her evening had gone. I never told her, and neither did he, that for the past two hours he'd been pacing nervously around the house. I didn't acknowledge it, even to him, but when she got home, he gave her a giant hug and said simply, "I'm glad you had a good time, kid. Oh, and you looked very beautiful tonight."

Still listening to the radio in the dark, I said a simple prayer for Francine's safety, for her happiness. I decided that sleeping was hopeless, so I turned on the lights and made a pot of tea. I began to straighten out the table, and I noticed a postcard in the stack of outgoing mail. A postcard? It had a picture of the Chicago skyline and on the back, written in Gary's handwriting, it said:

From Song of Songs 6:9—"But my dove, my perfect one, is unique, the only daughter of her mother, the favorite of the one who bore her. The maidens saw her and called her blessed."

Your mother misses you. I miss you. We're proud of you. We're blessed to have you in our lives.

Love, Dad

I sat with the postcard clenched to my heart. A tear of pride ran down my face. I poured myself a cup of tea and sat down at the table. *Yes, Francine, we're blessed to have you in our lives.*

CHAPTER 3

While You Were Out

Your word is like a lamp for my feet and a light for my path.
(Psalm 119:105).

A jangling phone. Whether it's an old-fashioned land line or a Bluetooth device beeping in your ear, it's bringing you an important message. It might be the voice of an old friend, a new business opportunity, a family crisis, or someone wishing you happy birthday. Or it could be something astounding that you didn't expect. And it might have come while you were out.

Angels on the Freeway

PAT J. SIKORA

D rat! Why now, Lord?" I fumed as my car sputtered and crawled to a stop. "You know I can't be without my car this week! Where are You when I need You?"

For months our nearly new sedan had been stalling, but the problem was so intermittent that I knew taking it in for service would be useless. Then the engine began knocking and stumbling, making the car almost undrivable.

This was just one more bit of evidence proving my growing certainty that God had gone on vacation and left me behind. A book deadline loomed before me. I was spending almost an hour each day shuttling my five-year-old son back and forth to Vacation Bible School. Meanwhile, my time with the Lord had become a barren desert. In fact, when I tried to meet Him each morning, I'd fall asleep over my Bible and coffee. It had been a long time since I had experienced any sign of His presence. And now I had to take the car in for service some twenty miles away and find a ride back home. What else could go wrong?

The next day at the dealer's service department I remembered another minor problem. I'd better have it checked. Otherwise, with my luck, I'd be back next week.

"By the way, sometimes when we brake, the car swerves a bit. It's been intermittent for the past six months or so, but maybe you can check it out," I said as an afterthought.

That afternoon, I got a call from the service manager. "Mrs. Sikora, the nuts that hold the K-frame to the steering mechanism are missing. That's why you're swerving. We've ordered a new K-frame, but that will take at least three days."

Before I could sputter my protest, he added, "But the good news is that even though your car is out of warranty, the manufacturer will cover it. That's a $750 job! They've never seen this problem on such a new car."

When I asked about the engine-stalling problem, he said the car was so dangerous that he wouldn't allow his technicians to test it until the K-frame was replaced. "You're lucky to be alive, Mrs. Sikora."

Then I realized that God had not been on vacation. In fact, His angels had been working overtime, securing that steering mechanism as my son and I rushed along the freeway twice each day. He had allowed the engine problem to worsen, motivating us to stop procrastinating and seek help. He had reminded me to mention the steering problem—something I had forgotten about. He had given the mechanic the wisdom to find an unusual problem. And He had motivated the manufacturer to save us a major expense. No, God was not on vacation. In fact, He was my present and active Protector. He had commanded His angels concerning me, to guard me in all my ways (Psalm 91:11).

True Poetry in Motion

ELIZABETH SCHMEIDLER

T*oday is the day to take your poems down to the Good Book Store.* The words rose up inside of me while I was doing my daily housework. Though the thought was unmistakable, I wondered if the idea was mine or God's. I suppose I was secretly hoping that the idea was mine to reject—especially since I really didn't feel the confidence or the inclination to expose my work in this type of public venue. However, within moments, my heart began to quicken as my mind reminded me of the phrase that I had grown so accustomed to saying to those who complimented my writing: "Thank you, but my writing comes from God, not me." The words seemed to float peacefully through the air, gently, but profoundly affirming what I knew to be true—my poetry was God's and not my own. It was to be shared. So, I resigned myself to giving the idea further thought.

The notion to sell my spiritual poetry at the local Christian book store was not a new one—several people had suggested it, and since I was a stay-at-home mom, I sincerely felt that God had blessed me with both a way to share His words of faith, hope, love, and comfort, as well as help my family a bit with financial provision. Still, even while I was packing my framed poems into a box, I was reluctant to peddle what God had so freely given me and argued the wisdom of what I was doing. To take my poems to a stranger and barter them just seemed unfathomable. In truth, I was petrified of the rejection. This was one of many times I had to remind myself that only God's will was important—only His opinion mattered. I continued selecting my favorite poems and carried them to the car.

The drive downtown took only minutes. I pulled up to the storefront and stared through the window. There were a few people milling about inside. Only seconds later, I pulled away from the curb and drove off. I just couldn't do it.

While waiting at the stoplight, my conscience worked on me. I headed back to the store, only to find that my parking spot was gone. *Must be a sign for me to go home . . . the manager probably isn't even in right now,* I thought hopefully. *The boys are by themselves and I've got to get dinner started.* These were all excuses and I knew it.

As I circled around the block for the third time, tears welled up in my eyes. *Please God, I just can't do this!* I was now trembling just a bit. Self-confidence had never been much of a part of my life, and insecurities and hurtful memories of past failures seemed to mock me. I began to pray for strength and peace. Within moments, the memories of all the times that God had shown me His strength and providence came flooding in. He reminded me of the courage and strength He had given me to sing solo in church, though I possessed no courage of my own. He reminded me of my husband, who was a gift and answered prayer that had poured out daily from my young heart. He reminded me of the blessed gift of my children and how He was helping me raise them, knowing that my own abilities would have been insufficient. He reminded me that He had a plan for me—I was *His* idea. He created me just the way He wanted me and gave me everything good that I ever possessed or would possess. I looked up to see a parking space opening up. It was time to dry my tears and walk through that door.

Without wasting another moment, I took a deep breath and asked for the manager. I told myself that it didn't matter a bit whether or not the manager wanted to buy my poetry. What was more important at that moment was for me to step out in faith and be obedient to God's call. Still, I found myself holding my breath as Normadine, the manager, walked up to me and I introduced myself. It was God who gave me the courage to speak—I was truly incapable of doing this on my own, and I knew it.

Normadine graciously smiled at me and began to

politely finger through the poems. At this writing, I can't remember if I was holding my breath while she read them, or chattering on and on like a ninny—both of which are distinct possibilities. What I do remember was that she asked me if I had anything that would comfort someone who had experienced the loss of a loved one. I pulled out my poem "You'll Know" and handed it to her. It took less than a minute for her to read it, but it felt like an eternity before she looked up at me with teary eyes and said, "This is beautiful. I have been looking high and low through my shop and my books trying to find something special for a woman who has just lost her mother. This will be perfect."

I remember turning into mush at that moment. My story about how I almost didn't come in because of my fear of rejection came rushing out of me. We both knew that God had sent me there on that day, at that perfect moment in time.

Several weeks later, Normadine called and was elated to tell me that a second copy of that same poem had been ordered and would be on its way to the country of Turkey as soon as I could get it there. I was astounded, and still am, at the thought that God could use me—a simple, small-town girl to convey a message that would travel and minister to a heart so very far away. Now, that's a God who truly cares!

God is amazing. He is always present, always working. His plan is perfect—His timing impeccable. He is

Lord of all things and has promised to be with us through every trial.

You'll Know

As you open your eyes to an "average" day,
a beautiful sunrise will brighten your way . . .
   and you'll know.

Amid the noise and confusion of life's hectic pace,
a bird will sing sweetly merely inches from your face . . .
   and you'll know.

When you're tired and lonely, or filled with despair,
the gentle voice of a friend will call through the air . . .
   and you'll know.

If you think I have left you, and can't feel Me near,
I will speak to your heart, listen quietly and hear . . .
   and you'll know.

You were Mine from the beginning, before I ever saw your face,
Let your heart feel My love as you're wrapped in
   My embrace . . .
   and you'll know.

—Elizabeth J. Schmeidler ©

Peanut Butter and Crackers

SAUNDRA KAY

P eanut butter? That's all we've got for supper?" My third, and youngest, child leaned against the kitchen counter and looked at me with disbelief. For all of his sixteen years, his big brown eyes had been notorious for beaming with happiness. Rarely ever had he cast as much concern as he did that day.

"There's some bread and some crackers in the pantry," I said, trying to sound natural so he wouldn't detect any strain in my voice. I walked over to the dishwasher, opened it up and pulled out a spoon. My motherly instinct assured me that my son was watching my back.

"Mama, there's no more food in the house? What are we going to do?"

Shame ripped my heart. Being unemployed and struggling to make ends meet for the past few months had been tough enough. But to stand before my child and tell him we had no food shattered me inside.

"Don't worry, baby. Every thing will work out fine. I promise." I patted him on the shoulder. "When you come in from school tomorrow, God will have blessed us with some food. You'll see."

While he opened the refrigerator and gazed at its emptiness, I untwisted a tie on the cellophane bag and pulled out the last two slices of bread. Opening a jar half-filled with peanut butter, I forced a smile. "If you eat a sandwich and drink a big glass of water, I'm sure that will hold you through the night."

"Well . . ." he said reluctantly, "I guess I'll settle for peanut butter on bread."

Pretending to be perfectly happy, I chirped, "Great! I'll make you a sandwich, and I'll eat peanut butter and crackers."

Later that night after I'd retired to my room, my son walked in and sat at the foot of my bed. His eyes roamed the walls as if to keep from looking directly at me.

"Mama, you said that God will give us some food, but . . . are . . . are you sure?"

Hearing the fear in my child's voice and witnessing the pitiful look on his face caused my heart to ache worse than a tooth cavity. I closed the book I was reading and focused my undivided attention on him.

"I'm absolutely sure. Son, God knows we have no food. And He knows I have no money. He also knows that we strive hard in this house to live according to His will."

My baby boy looked as if he was about to cry.

I climbed out of bed and walked around and sat next to him. "God wouldn't dare withhold from us the things we need most." I struggled to remain calm as I prayed within for God to comfort my child. "He is not about to let us starve."

"But how do you know that for sure, Mama?" His eyes begged for assurance.

Just as I opened my mouth to speak, I received a revelation. I grabbed my Bible from the nightstand and flipped it open to the book of Psalms.

"Look here, son. Let's read this together." I placed the Bible between the two of us and pointed to Psalm 37:25, and then we read: "I have been young, and now am old; yet have I not seen the righteous forsaken, nor his seed begging bread" (KJV).

"So does that mean we won't have to beg anybody for bread, and that God will give us some anyway?" My son's concern was far too advanced for his young age.

Trying desperately to hide my hurt inside, I quickly answered, "Exactly!"

As soon as he left my room to prepare for bed, I cried out to the Lord. "Please, God, help me."

The next morning as I sat at the dining table eating a handful of peanut butter-filled crackers and gazing out the window, I was pleasantly surprised to see a beautiful redbird resting on the sill. My elders claimed that a redbird's visit meant company was coming. Maybe so, but I decided the little birdie brought a message to me.

Immediately, I opened my Bible to a favorite passage in the sixth chapter of Matthew. When I got to verse 26, where it says, "Look at the birds of the air; they do not sow or reap or store away in barns, and yet your heavenly Father feeds them . . ." (NIV), I felt certain the red bird was a reminder straight from above.

Feeling that God was watching over me, I closed my eyes and prayed. "Lord, have mercy . . . please provide food for my family."

Right before I said "amen," I heard the phone ringing. Normally, I wouldn't have interrupted my prayer to answer the phone. And I almost didn't then. But I had a strong inclination to do so. I moved to the end of the kitchen counter and picked up the phone.

"Hello."

"Hi, Sweetie," my mother's keen voice greeted me from the other end of the line.

"Good morning, Mama."

"Guess where we're getting ready to go?"

Oh my goodness! In the midst of worrying, I had forgotten that Mama and Daddy were coming to visit for the weekend. My parents lived almost two hundred miles from me and rarely drove out to visit. Whenever they did come, we always had a big celebration.

Lord, what do I do now? The weekend is only two

days away. I don't have food for my children, let alone Mama and Daddy. Focusing so hard on food, I almost missed what she said next.

"Your daddy and I were wondering, since we don't have any plans for the next couple of days, would it be okay if we drove out today and stayed two extra days?"

Not wanting my parents to know my situation, I had no choice but to trust God.

"Sure, Mama, I'd love that. We'll have a wonderful time," I answered with as much enthusiasm as I could muster.

"And another thing," Mama continued, "your sister and her girls want to come with us and . . ."

I fell over into the nearby chair as Mama's words faded into the background.

Lord, what am I going to do? How am I supposed to feed a house full of people for four days—with no food?

When I recovered from my shock, Mama—bless her heart—was steady rattling. "Your sister says since you're providing a place for all of us to stay, she'll buy the food. So just wait 'till we get there to go grocery shopping."

Oh, thank You, God, I cried within. I hurried up and finished talking to Mama and hung up the phone, so I could rejoice. "Hallelujah! God, You did it!"

Soon after my family arrived, my sister and I went shopping. We bought plenty of everything, including chips and dips, cookies and ice cream, popcorn and peanuts and candy, milk and soda and juice, fruits and vegetables, steaks and chickens, hot dogs and hamburgers, bacon and sausage, eggs and rice, biscuits and sweet rolls, and—of course—more peanut butter and crackers.

That afternoon when my son came home from school, all kinds of food awaited him. Food covered the counter tops, food was stacked on top of the table, and food was packed in the pantry. He was so surprised all he could do was stand there and stare. *Now I know God will,* his eyes seemed to say.

To this day, I'm still eating peanut butter and crackers. Rarely a week goes by (most times not even a couple of days) without my indulging in my favorite snack. Sure, I really like peanut butter and crackers. But more, I absolutely love the supernatural nourishment I receive each time I bite into my hallowed snack. Instead of simply eating peanut butter and crackers, I'm tasting . . . and seeing . . . all of the goodness God has given me. It's like a constant reminder of our God's powerful promise, "O taste and see that the Lord is good: blessed is the man that trusteth in him."

The $32,000 Question

CATHARINE R. KIM

Y ou're kidding!" Incredulous, I stared at my husband across our cluttered living room, where we were sorting out things before the movers came. "You've got to be kidding," I repeated. "You mean we pray and ask God for money?"

"Why not?" asked Dick reasonably. The Bible tells us God provides for all our needs, and right now we need money.

I was skeptical. "Suppose we pray and nothing happens?"

"Something always happens when we pray," Dick persisted, "Whatever the prayer, God answers. Sometimes He says yes, sometimes He says no, and at other times He says wait. This time," he added positively, "I think He'll answer yes, because He's already opened the door, by having you call back to appear on *The $128,000 Question.*"

I wanted to believe him, but couldn't. All my Puritan New England upbringing rebelled against the idea. We pray to God to give us strength to do our duty or for courage to bear our burdens, but we make and lie in our own financial beds. "God helps those who help themselves" was a frequently used expression in my childhood home. "God gave you intelligence and a healthy body," I'd often been told. "The rest is up to you."

The $128,000 Question, aired in the United States and Canada, is a nighttime television quiz show for experts on various subjects. Twice the previous winter we had flown to New York with high hopes that I, chosen as a contestant expert on Agatha Christie, would be called to appear. I was on the show briefly as a filler at the end of the season, but had not been asked even one question. At the time I was told that if the show was renewed for the 1977 fall season, I'd probably hear by no later than the end of April. But as April turned into May, and May became June, I put away the books I had studied for so long and decided to put the show out of my mind. My dream of winning enough money to pay off the $10,000 second mortgage on our home died.

And I had benefitted from the experience. In common, I suppose, with many other women, I had been made uneasy and vaguely guilty by the women's liberation movement. Was I missing something by being just a housewife and mother? Ought I to be expanding my horizons, discovering my "true" identity? Those weeks of intensive studying, when I isolated myself from Dick and the children, resolved my doubts. I knew what I wanted. I resented the fact that the studying robbed me of precious time with my family; a walk around our untended house showed me more clearly than a dozen self-discovery magazine articles that I did have a "true" identity, that of being the hub of the household from which Dick and the children radiated like spokes into their outside worlds—Dick to the Episcopal church of which he was rector, the five children still living at home to their various schools. I hadn't won money, but I'd won something far more valuable—contentment and a sense of my own worth.

The television show was forgotten, and summer brought the new excitement of a move to Hawaii from our home in Alabama. Dick was called to be rector of the Episcopal Church of the Good Shepherd, in Wailuku on the island of Maui and enthusiastically accepted. I was not only unenthusiastic, I was nearly frantic with worry. That second mortgage, we had been warned, could create real difficulties in the sale of our house, and although the new parish had given us an extremely generous moving allowance, I suspected that for a family the size of ours, it was far from adequate. An estimate from the local mover confirmed my fears. Somehow, out of our own pocket, we were going to have to find an additional $5000 to cover our moving expenses.

"We'll go bankrupt!" I wailed. "Two mortgages, and where on earth are we going to get $5000?"

"God will find the way," Dick said serenely.

I'd turned angrily away. *Dick,* I thought resentfully, *relied on God to produce $5000 and pay off a second mortgage, and then forgot the matter. He left me to do the worrying.*

The telephone call from *The $128,000 Question* on that August morning, ten days before we left Alabama, came as a total surprise. The show had relocated to Canada, I was told. Could Dick and I be in Toronto the following Monday, when tapings for the fall season were to begin?

I couldn't refuse, despite the inconvenience. After all, I might win something, and we surely needed it. Now here was Dick, not simply hoping, but confidently telling me we should pray for what we needed and that unless God had another plan for meeting those needs, I would win.

"I might not even be called!" I protested.

"You'll be called," Dick said.

I continued to protest. Our small town lacked many of the books I had needed, and although I was fairly sure of my ability to answer questions about Agatha Christie's mystery novels, I knew I was weak in other areas, especially her plays.

"I don't even know all the titles of her plays, or when they opened," I reminded Dick. "If I'm questioned about them, I'll lose."

Dick reminded me of those months of hard studying; couldn't I trust in God to do the rest?

Full of anticipation, we flew to Toronto. Dick's belief that this time I would be called to appear was correct. I was chosen for the first show, but as I stood in the wings waiting to be called on stage, confidence fled from me. I am a painfully shy person, and the thought of doing the one thing I most dread, appearing publicly before a group of strangers, terrified me. I was trembling with fright as the pretty hostess led me onto the set and introduced me to host Alex Trebek. Mr. Trebek is a warm and friendly man who must have had to draw heavily on his expertise as I whispered brief answers to his casual questions about myself and Dick, the children, and my interest in Agatha Christie.

Answering the quiz questions was easier. By pretending I was back in school, taking an examination, I could forget the live audience. That night we taped three shows, at the end of which I had reached the $8000 plateau.

Old habits die hard, and I had slipped back to relying on myself instead of trusting in God. The emotional and mental strain had been intense; I wasn't sure I could take another day of it. Still nervous and frightened, I talked over the next day's tapings with Dick.

"If I try for $16,000 and lose," I argued, "we'll go home with the consolation prize of a new car which will be useless to us. The $8000, even with taxes, at least will pay our moving expenses."

"What have we been praying for?" Dick asked quietly.

"All right," I agreed. "I'll make an act of faith. Let's figure out what we need."

Because of taxes, and because a part of the winnings is in the form of prizes, to get the $15,000 we needed I would have to reach the $32,000 plateau. I doubted repeatedly, and as often renewed my act of faith.

Somehow, his words turned everything around for me. The decision I was trying to make was not really about the show, it was about God. I had a choice to make, a terribly important one. I could choose to place absolute trust in God, or I could choose to live out the rest of my days with a God whom I would let into my head, but not into my daily life. I wanted Him in my life! Of course I would continue with the show. God's answer to our prayer might be no; if it was, we'd accept our disappointment and wait in confidence for His will to be revealed.

The next morning we wandered through one of Toronto's malls, killing time until the noonday service at the Cathedral, which we'd attended on each of our days in Canada. In a bookstore I noticed a bibliography I'd not yet come across, and bought it for my rapidly expanding Christie collection.

It was too late to do any more studying, but after

church I leafed through the book and in it discovered information new to me, two pages which listed all the plays Agatha Christie wrote, their opening dates, and the original titles of those taken from novels or short stories. I read the list through, and then put the book away. What happened tonight was in God's hands, not mine.

That evening I felt relaxed and easy. A new presence was with me on the set. Although no one could see Him, I knew that God was there.

I reached the $16,000 plateau without difficulty, but when I stood in the isolation booth for the $32,000 questions, my face must have shown panic and dismay.

"Agatha Christie wrote many plays . . ." began Mr. Trebek.

Right then, I knew I had lost. Except for those two brief pages in the book I'd bought that morning, I knew next to nothing about Agatha Christie's plays. I began to plan ahead to the moment when I would step out of the isolation booth, thinking of words which would show the audience what a "good loser" I could be. Then I remembered what Dick had said earlier about my having done my part by studying; I still had a part to play, and I forced my mind back to Mr. Trebek, as he began reading the six questions I would have to answer. I listened carefully, and began to believe in miracles. Almost all of the questions contained references to original titles of plays or their opening dates. Although ordinarily I do not have a photographic memory, I could see the answers from the book as clearly as though God Himself were holding it open before me. I missed a question that dealt with plot, but was allowed a make-up question which I correctly answered.

God had done it! He'd said yes to our prayers! We could start the new ministry in Hawaii free from the crippling burden of financial worries.

I appeared on one more show, to announce my decision not to try to reach the $64,000 level and become the season's first big winner. I was tempted to continue, but I felt it would be wrong. God had answered our prayers; I couldn't take matters back into my own hands. I've never seen the show I was on, so I don't remember exactly what I said. I think it was something like this:

"God has given us exactly what we prayed for. Without further guidance from Him, and I've received none, I cannot continue."

For a few months I cherished a dream or two—that taxes might not take as much as we'd been warned, that there might be a little left over, that I wouldn't have to sell the car I'd received as part of my winnings. I learned another valuable lesson: God doesn't necessarily give us what we want, but only what we need. When we had paid off the second mortgage, set aside money for taxes, paid the mover and absorbed the inevitable costs that accompany settling into a new house, there was just enough money left to pay the tithe of thanksgiving which we had vowed to give from our winnings to be used to glorify God.

The fun, the excitement and the money are all things of the past. What remains is the permanent knowledge that God does care about us, that our problems are as real to Him as they are to us, and that when we pray and trust, He leads us through the difficult times in order to free us to do His work.

You'll Never Guess What We're Studying

JOYCE L. VEDRAL

I almost gasped at the thought that entered my mind during our teachers' meeting that afternoon at Julia Richman High School in New York City.

The department chairman had called all the English teachers together. She was concerned about the students' growing boredom with traditional English courses. Class-skipping was frequent.

"Can any of you offer something special in English?" she asked. This was when what seemed like a shocking idea came to me as if it were an inspiration from heaven. I knew the Bible well; why not offer to teach it as literature?

I made the suggestion, then held my breath. I was well aware of the controversy over religion in school. "Fine!" said the chairman, "make up a course, find students willing to take it, and it's all yours."

Thus my experiment began. Julia Richman has a mixture of black, white, and Spanish teenagers. How could I get those often indifferent students interested enough to sign up for the course?

On the morning I was to approach the students, I prayed for the right words. Then I stood before the first of many classes and said, "I'm here to offer you a new course in place of regular senior English—The Bible as Literature."

The students groaned, gasped, and giggled.

Bravely I continued. "Many of you will be going to college. You will find that the Bible is frequently quoted in English literature. Poetry is filled with references to it; so are novels and plays."

I stopped for a moment. The class was quiet. "Who can tell me who the first slaves in the Bible were?"

Silence.

"Who built the ark?" A few hands went up.

I could sense interest building.

"Do you know what the Bible says about how the world will end?"

The kids sat up in their seats.

I went on. "Do you know what the Bible says about witchcraft and fortunetelling?"

Now the class became noisy with students discussing the questions, speculating about answers.

"This is not going to be a Sunday school class," I said. "We can discuss and even argue about religion. You can laugh and take it as a joke. That is your affair. My point is simply this: Do you want to be an educated person? If so, then how can you not know a little about the best-read Book in the world?"

By now I was being interrupted by students asking how to sign up. I went on to challenge twelve English classes in this same way. By the time I finished, sixty students had signed up for what was then called Bible One.

I spent the summer developing the course. I decided to teach the books of Genesis and Exodus, Ruth, Psalms and Proverbs, then go into Matthew, John, Romans, Corinthians, and Revelation. I made up sheets for homework assignments and class discussion starters. They went something like this: "Why did God ask Abraham to kill his only son, Isaac?" Answer: "A test of faith, illustrating that God demands a person's first allegiance, his or her will."

After I started teaching the course in September, 1970, there were some surprises. I quickly discovered that my students were not impressed with the parallelisms in Proverbs or the epic cycles in Genesis. But they did listen carefully when we discussed the Bible's stand on witchcraft, homosexuality, premarital sex, and Judgment Day.

So I salted the course to their interests. As a result, my students were so eager to discuss their ideas that when the bell rang, a general moan arose. As they filed out, they would still be discussing their ideas.

Since they were fascinated with witchcraft, we did an extensive Bible study on the subject. Many misconceptions were peeled away; questions were answered.

They eagerly tackled a series of book reports on works like Melville's *Moby Dick*, Hawthorne's *The Scarlet Letter*, relating them specifically to the Bible.

In presenting the biblical material, I tried to offer both sides of the argument and let the students freely battle it out. For example, we discussed the parting of the Red Sea. Some scholars, I said, claimed that there were winds that would sometimes press back the shallow waters there. Could it have been a lucky break for the Hebrews? The students got the point: If one isn't inclined to believe in miracles, one can find grounds to doubt; if one wants to believe, one can find evidence for the other side.

One day while I was teaching a lesson about the miracles of Christ, the chairman of the English department came into the room to observe. I wondered about her reaction.

After the students left, she said, "When I heard the students raving about how much they were learning, I could hardly believe it. In fact, I was afraid of being disappointed. But I wasn't, not at all."

She looked out the window at the skyline, which the afternoon sun was touching with gold. "The aim of your lesson as I saw it," she went on thoughtfully, "was the extent to which faith is involved in a miracle. I was happy to see that almost everyone took part in the discussion."

She turned back to me and smiled, "This course proves what we have always believed: If you offer a student something in which he's interested, he'll attend class, do his reading, take an active part."

At the end of the term, out of the sixty students, only two failed, and they both had attended class only once. But passing grades were not the only rewards. One girl wrote in a composition: "I had never really thought about life and death before. I had never asked myself what I believe in. Now I know that I believe in Jesus, that He is my salvation."

Seven students approached me to ask about attending church. Others came with personal problems, asking how the Bible could help in solving them.

After the first course, some of my students circulated a petition to have it extended to Bible Two. In the spring term, eighty students signed up for Bible One and thirty from my first class continued on to Bible Two.

Bible Two added a new dimension to the material. The students gave oral reports on different denominations, sects, and Eastern religions. If they preferred, they could get a speaker from the particular religion to come and talk to the class instead of speaking themselves.

Our first speaker happened to be a Catholic priest. One girl said later, "I saw God in him." Next we had two Jehovah's Witnesses. Some of the students got into a lively argument with them, quoting Scripture of which they had known nothing six months previously. Then a Baptist minister came; he finished his talk with an invitation to his church.

Some students who went on to college reported back to say how much Bible study had helped them, from giving them an easy familiarity with biblical references in English literature to preparation for college-level religion courses.

The Bible as Literature could be offered in most schools. Since starting the course, I have learned that there is no question about the legality of it. A Supreme Court decision stated that Bible reading for the purpose of education is to be encouraged, not discouraged, as long as it is taught as literature.

In New York City, several other high schools are now offering a course similar to mine to their students. Moreover, inquiries about how to go about planning such a course are coming to me from many high schools around the country; several have already instituted it.

Of course, it has all meant extra time and work for me. But then, what kind of English teacher would I be if I didn't introduce my students to the best-read classic in world literature?

A Delightful Message

SUE FERGUSON

My dark eyes gazed with frustration at the framed picture. Hanging on the sunny yellow wall of our master bedroom, it was the first thing I saw each morning and the last thing that caught my eye every evening as I wearily slid between the sheets under the time-worn patchwork quilt covering our bed. Just inside the metallic gold frame, colorful, hand-stitched flowers bordered the Bible verse: "Delight thyself in the Lord; and he shall give thee the desires of thine heart" (Psalm 37:4). Though innocent, simple cross-stitches on woven cloth, that wall hanging seemed deceptive. I read it over and over again. Angrily I wondered: *Haven't I delighted in the Lord? Why don't I have the desires of my heart? Well, I g-u-ess I do, except for one . . .*

As a child, going home to an empty house after school was frightening. Because of my routine searches under the beds and in the closets for boogeymen, I resolved to be a stay-at-home wife and mother when I grew up. My children, instead of entering a scary house, would have the security of my presence and a friendly hug to greet them. Warm, melt-in-your-mouth cookies would be a tasty perk too!

Before our move I'd been able to stay home and earn a little supplemental income from hobbies and home interests. My most recent cottage industry had been a subscription newsletter entitled *At Home: Simple encouragement and practical advice for those whose hearts are at home.* But now we lived in one of the most expensive counties in the United States, just north of San Francisco, and I needed a real job. Before I knew it, I had one. My twelve-hour-a-week, part-time job threatened to become twelve hours a day! Life wasn't matching my ideal dream, and I was sinking with the weight of my disappointment and the demands on my busy schedule.

With doubt directed toward the God I had thoughtfully followed since early childhood, I read that verse morning after morning and night after night with despair. *Lord, You aren't giving me the desire of my heart, and I'm not all that delighted with You!*

With one child in middle school and two in high school, we were constantly attending music programs and athletic events. As the pastor's family we hosted church activities at our house four times each week. Success at work meant the responsibilities and challenges of my job were increasing and travel became routine. I liked what I did, the products and the people I worked with—but my heart was at home, and I never seemed to be there. *What about the desire of my heart, Lord?*

I hated my life even though I knew my circumstances were what many women would have envied. My husband helped immensely with household and family responsibilities; he even cooked dinner most nights. With a healthy marriage, three well-adjusted teenagers, caring friends, and a thriving career, what was my problem? My circumstances were good, but I was miserable.

All through those dark days I was actively participating in church activities, reading my Bible almost daily, and praying consistently, if you can call constant whining aimed at God prayer! I even desperately visited a Christian counselor. I spent eighty dollars to hear, "You can't even imagine how many other Christian women in leadership roles also struggle with the demanding lifestyle here!"

A-a-a-a-g-h! Maybe misery loves company, but I left that counselor's office feeling gypped. I wanted help, a solution to the bondage I felt, and she offered me none.

One evening during the intermission of a high school music performance, another mother brought me a shopping bag filled with fabric, a pattern, and all the notions needed to make my daughter's costume for an upcoming musical. The remainder of the program, I struggled to contain the tears and frustration that threatened to explode! *Lord I know it's just one costume, for my own daughter, but I can't . . . I just can't do one more thing!*

Normal responsibilities annoyed me and I wondered if life was even worth living. I lingered . . . *What would happen if I wasn't here? I hate my life! No, stop thinking this way, my family needs me, but I can't go on like this!* Each time I tried to talk to a friend about my overwhelming schedule, they would respond by telling me how busy they were. The counselor hadn't helped, my friends offered no sympathy, and my husband was already helping as much as he possibly could. *God, where are You?*

While suffering in the dark hole of my despair, my husband and I met longtime friends for lunch at a local Chinese restaurant. They were just passing through town. Bev, my God-fearing friend and prayer partner from years past, shared some personal health struggles and then, after a deep breath, boldly declared, "I will not allow Satan to rob me of my joy."

Oblivious to the rest of the lunchtime conversation, I sat quietly, holding tight to her words as though they were a life preserver tossed across the table to rescue me. *Is that what I've done Lord? Have I allowed the enemy to rob me of my joy?* My mind replayed that statement, "I will not allow Satan to rob me of my joy," over and over again for days, months, and even now, years later it still comes to my mind often.

That was my problem! Unconscious of the thief, I had allowed my joy to be stolen. Bev's words replayed in my thoughts, and the wall hanging, "Delight thyself in the Lord and he shall give thee the desires of thine heart," spoke God's instruction and promise for retrieving it into my weary heart.

But I had developed a pattern of negative thoughts, all focusing on poor little ol' me. *I hate my life; I never have time to do anything I want to do. I can't even keep up with the things I'm supposed to do!* Each day as I drove off to work, past neighbors walking their dogs, I wondered why I couldn't be out walking. *It's just not fair! I want to walk my dog too . . .*

Bev had helped me identify the problem, but the negative thoughts continued. Knowing I needed to make a deliberate choice, I clung to the words in that cross-stitch wall hanging: "Delight thyself in the Lord; and he shall give thee the desires of thine heart." The appropriate prescription for my joy-robbed heart surely must be a large daily dose of delighting in the Lord. Desperate, I set out to see if God would keep His promise! *If I delight in You, will You really give me the desires of my heart?*

The half-hour commute I had resented became five hours of Scripture memory time each week; I focused on verses about the heart and said them out loud and with expression until they penetrated deep into my hurting heart and overtook my depressing thoughts. Rather than work through lunch, four days each week I packed a healthy meal and drove to a nearby parking lot. After eating I spent the remainder of my lunch hour seeking God wholeheartedly, searching His Word for truths to combat the enemy's hold; on Fridays I went to lunch with co-workers. Soon I began to program my phone for breaks I had previously been too busy to take and went outside briefly at least once during each workday.

Gradually I found time to begin walking my lab three miles several evenings a week. I soaked up the fresh, moderate climate and reviewed my Scripture memory as he and I relished in the beauty of the San Francisco Bay area.

Finally, after several months of large daily doses of delighting in the Lord, I heard myself laugh out loud. Initially startled, I was soon overcome with relief. *That felt good! It's been so long.* I experienced the truth: "'You will seek me and find me when you seek me with all your heart. I will be found by you,' declares the Lord, 'and will bring you back from captivity'" (Jeremiah 29:13–14 NIV).

My circumstances didn't change; they had been good all along. They just weren't consistent with my expectations. No longer was I a slave to my disappointments and negative thoughts; God freed me with Himself. My self-centered focus shifted to the incredible Almighty God and my heart's desire was Him!

My perspective, previously blinded by my joy-robbed heart, saw with fresh, joy-filled eyes. God had provided my children a secure and welcome homecoming after school. Not only did they have each other's companionship, my husband's office was in our home. The job I liked but didn't really think I wanted provided generously for our family's needs, taught me new skills, and cultivated lifelong friendships. God put me on a path to fulfill heart desires I hadn't yet discovered, or even imagined! He used His Word to transform my wants and prepare me for a future filled with writing and speaking opportunities.

Several years have passed since God spoke to me through that cross-stitched verse: "Delight thyself in the Lord; and he shall give thee the desires of thine heart." I look back with awe and gratefulness! God has generously given me the desires of His heart and made them mine. Large daily doses of enjoying Him continue to fill my heart with joy. When home I'm often writing at my computer or preparing messages for travel days. I thrill at every opportunity to encourage others to "delight in Him!"

Searching Normandy

REBECCA S. RAMSEY

I drew in my raincoat against the chill as I followed my parents and my brother across the grounds of the Normandy American Military Cemetery in Colleville-sur-Mer, France. *What's wrong with me?* I asked myself. This should have been a heart-pounding moment for my whole family. Surely it was for Mom. For the first time in her life, she would stand at the grave of her father, Glen Edward Kuhn, a man she never really knew. He was killed in World War II on Mom's first birthday, July 29, 1944, and visiting his gravesite was something she had always wanted to do. A good daughter would be right by her side, but standing there in an ocean of headstones I just wished I could wait in the car.

Seeing Omaha Beach had been hard enough. It made me sick to my stomach to imagine those men—boys, really—storming out of the water that lapped so quietly at my feet. So many of them never left Normandy and are now laid out in military precision under that green lawn, marked by thousands of marble crosses and Stars of David. I read the names and dates on marker after marker and did quick calculations of the years from birth to death. Robert, William, John—those strangers who shared the names of some of my friends at school were my age, nineteen.

My stomach was knotted for those boys and for their families, too, because I knew my mother's loss. It would be hard enough to lose your father, but to have him taken on your birthday! Even though Grandma remarried, and Granddaddy Farley loved Mom as one of his own, birthdays must have always been tinged with a little sadness. After the cake had been eaten and the night had grown still, she must have thought of her father, wondering what his laughter sounded like, how he had walked across a room, and what he'd thought of his baby girl.

I was sad for my mom, but it wasn't just sadness I felt. My stomach hurt for my own guilt and frustration as well. Standing before those headstones, I could hear my own life's minutes ticking by. Each of those boys had made such a profound contribution to the world, laying down their lives for what they believed in. I, on the other hand, was lucky enough to have a whole future ahead of me, and yet I couldn't seem to choose any direction for my life. What contribution would I make?

My friends seemed to have their whole lives planned out. But me? My biochemistry degree was halfway done, and I still didn't know what I wanted to do with it—if anything. I knew that I wanted to serve God in some way, but how? My future plans reached only as far as the end of the summer. The moment we got home from France, I'd be repacking the car and heading out for a summer job as a youth minister in rural North Carolina. Would the ministry be my calling? What about teaching? If only God would make it clear how He wished me to serve!

As we walked to the visitors' center, Mom talked nervously and fingered the bouquet of flowers we'd bought for her father's grave. Inside the center, a slender young woman behind the desk welcomed us with a warm smile. She couldn't have been much older than I was. Her long, brown hair was pulled back into a ponytail, and her eyes were kind and sincere. Her English lilted with a French accent as she greeted us and then asked, "And what is the soldier's name?"

"Glen Edward Kuhn," my mother answered. "My father died on July 29, 1944." I could hear the slight tremble in her voice.

The woman looked through her book to find his name and then pointed on a map. "His grave is here," she said. "I would be honored to take you there." At our nod, she picked up a pail and a cloth from behind the desk, and Mom followed her, then my father and my brother and I. Our raincoats whipped around us in the wind. A quiet rain began as we turned down his row, searching the headstones for his name.

The young lady stopped, and we all fixed our eyes on the name on the cross. Our guide stood to the side while Mom and the rest of us read and reread the words:

GLEN E. KUHN

S SGT 83 QM CO 83 DIV

TENNESSEE JULY 29, 1944

After a quiet moment, our guide set her pail and cloth next to the cross. Gathering her skirt to one side, she knelt in front of the cross, pressing her bare knees into the wet grass. As the wind blew her hair about, she scooped up clumps of wet sand and rubbed them into the grooves of the carved lettering with her fingers, as gently as if she was putting ointment on a wound. She moved with quiet reverence, but what was she doing? It just seemed to make a dirty mess on the cross.

I looked to Dad for explanation. He stood close to Mom, watching. No one spoke.

When every groove was covered, she picked up the clean cotton cloth and rubbed it over the cross, slowly, gingerly brushing off the scattered sand. The wet sand left in the lettering was like a dark brown paint on the freshly polished cross. In an ocean of white gravestones, my grandfather's name stood out from them all.

As we drew closer to examine her work, she gathered her things and then shook each of our hands, thanking us for his sacrifice. I wish I could remember her words, because they were sincere and kind, but over the years they've slipped away. But what remains in my memory, as clearly as if it had happened only a moment ago, is the reverential way in which she knelt down in front of that cross to serve my mother and my family—and my grandfather. She was no pastor or missionary, but she surely ministered to us. As she filled in the letters on that cross, God was writing his own words on my heart: "This is how to serve me, Becky. Do all that you do with respect and humility and love, as if you were doing it for me."

The day after we returned from France, I began my summer of youth ministry. Although I loved the kids, the Bible studies, and even the car washes and bowling marathons, it was not the end of my career search. In fact I'm still searching. I've enjoyed plenty of work opportunities—as a chemist in a lab, a high school chemistry teacher, a camp director, a volunteer, and a mom. Though my career path has been a meandering trail more than a brightly lit road, God has given me a good traveling guide in the example of that young French woman. I've tried to follow her example of humble service in whatever job I'm doing.

Along my winding route, God has sprinkled in a few surprises. Though I never imagined I'd go back to France, my husband and I ended up moving there, to the little village of Aubiére, just a day's drive away from the

Normandy cemetery and beaches. And July 29th, which had always been a special day on my calendar, is now circled for yet another reason. Eight years after touring that cemetery, on July 29, 1992, my mom received an extra-special birthday gift. Her first grandson, my son Benjamin, was determined to arrive on his grandmother's birthday, several days past his due date!

So a day that was once tinged with sadness has now been blessed with hope. It illustrates to me once again that I needn't worry about the details of my life—as long as I'm willing to follow God, He'll lead me where I need to go.

My Greatest Thanksgiving

NANCY B. GIBBS

A re you going grocery shopping today?" my husband, Roy asked when I picked up the telephone. "I plan to," I answered.

Thanksgiving was only a couple days away. Everyone in our family would be coming to our house. My funds were limited; therefore my box of coupons awaited me in the car. I knew I had to be creative in my shopping that day. I had to stretch every dollar.

For a few seconds, Roy sat silently on the other end of the line. "Why do you ask?" I uttered, fearing what he might say.

"Nancy, there's a family with a half dozen kids that will not have anything to eat for Thanksgiving. The little one is only five-years-old."

"So what are you saying?" I whispered.

"While you're at the store, could you possibly buy something for them?" Roy's words echoed in my heart. Groceries, a five-year-old, eight in the family. My head began to spin thinking about the fifty dollars I had reserved for our family's Thanksgiving dinner. In the back of my mind I counted the hungry guests who would be coming to our house for dinner. I put my head down on my desk, already feeling defeated.

There's no way possible, I thought. But the compassion I heard in my husband's voice struck a nerve inside me.

"Sure," I replied. "But only if God helps."

"Thanks, sweetheart," Roy whispered. "Just do what you can." He then hung up the telephone. I finished my work and prayed all the way to the nearest grocery store. As I entered the parking lot, I noticed a big sign in the grocery store window: Turkeys—29 cents a pound.

"This is the place, Lord," I whispered. I grabbed my box of coupons, went inside, secured two buggies, and headed to the frozen foods. The turkeys were indeed on sale, but I discovered one big problem. When I read the sign posted on the freezer door my heart sank. "Limit one."

"But I need two," I uttered to myself. I decided to find the manager. I explained the problem. He made an exception. After tossing a turkey in each buggy, I began my shopping fury. It was amazing how many buy-one-get-one-free items were being featured that day. The first item went into one buggy. The free item went in the other. In addition, I had all the right coupons to get exactly what both families needed for a hearty Thanksgiving dinner.

I finally proceeded to the register and held my breath while the cashier rang up my groceries. To my surprise,

I had enough money. I was even able to purchase a package of cookies for the five-year-old who had stolen my heart, even though I had never met her.

Later that afternoon, Roy and I made a special delivery to a home filled with children of all ages. I will never forget the smiles on the six kids' faces as they made several trips from my car carrying numerous bags of groceries inside.

This event reminded me of a story. Even though He only had a few loaves and fishes, Jesus multiplied them and fed five thousand people. And to top it off, there was food left over. I wondered if God was doing the same thing that day.

By far, that was the greatest Thanksgiving Day of my life. My entire family shared a hearty meal with us. We had plenty to eat. We even had enough food left over for the evening meal.

That afternoon, when I had time to think about what had happened, I imagined a home, not far from where I lived. There was a mother and a father and six children sitting around the kitchen table, laughing and rejoicing. They enjoyed the same meal that our family had shared together that day.

Then I realized that miracles happen when we step out in faith, and in steps God. For with us, some things are impossible. "But with God, all things are possible" (Matthew 19:26 NIV).

CHAPTER 4

A Friendly Reminder

Hear the word of the LORD; listen to the teaching of our God! (Isaiah 1:10).

A friendly reminder is the string around your finger. It's the red circle on your calendar or your cell phone beeping to jog your memory about an important meeting. Sometimes God sends us friendly reminders too. They come in the form of amazing messages delivered in a variety of ways. Miraculous ways.

The Treasure

JOANNA GAINES

In 2000, my senior year at Baylor University in Waco, Texas, I was offered an internship in New York at CBS with Dan Rather. It was the most exciting opportunity I had ever dreamed of getting. So I prepared to make the move.

I was very close to my parents, so the thought of leaving them for six months was very sad. The day before I left, my precious father handed me a Bible with my name on it and a note inside addressed to me with my nickname "JoJo." It talked about how he would be praying for me and how excited he was that I was taking this opportunity to spread my wings. This Bible was my father's way of releasing me to go out on my own under the covering of my heavenly Father.

I read that Bible every day and I cherished it so. After my internship I moved back from New York to Waco to finish school. About a year later, my best friend, Jessica, was going on a Christian outreach trip to Boston for two weeks. She asked to borrow my Bible because the size was good for travel. I was reluctant, but I felt the Spirit of God say, "Release it to her." I handed it to her and explained that this was one of my most treasured possessions and to please take care of it.

She came back two weeks later almost in tears and told me she had lost my Bible and had no idea where it was. My heart dropped but I tried not to lose it in front of her, because I knew she already felt so badly. We prayed together and asked God to help the Bible find its way back to me somehow.

As I was driving home, I complained to God, "You know I treasured that Bible so much; why would You allow her to lose it? I listened to You and now it's gone." I felt His still, small voice say, "One day you will understand; maybe someone truly needs it more than you." At His whisper, I was silenced. I suddenly felt complete peace, and I truly let it go.

Six years later, I was married with two children, and I still thought of that Bible often. I was at my routine breakfast stop with my husband and kids a few weeks ago, and I heard a man say, "Joanna, come sit down. I want to share a story with you."

I remembered this man from our church a few years before. His name was Jeff Bianchi, and he had been helping plant a church in Boston for about seven years. Jeff said that during that seven years he had been talking to a friend about God. Jeff pursued him on a regular basis and prayed for his salvation. A few months ago the man finally chose Christ, and Jeff was so taken by God's faithfulness.

Jeff and his friend met one morning at a Dunkin Donuts for a visit. Jeff noticed that his friend pulled out a little black Bible with the name Joanna Stevens on it. Jeff said, "Where did you find that Bible?" His friend told Jeff he had found it years ago at a coffee shop and that for five years the little Bible had answered his questions about God.

Jeff looked at it and said, "I think I know this person." He opened the Bible and saw "Dear JoJo." Jeff pulled out his phone, called a friend in Waco and asked, "What does Joanna's dad call her?" It was confirmed that this was, without a doubt, my precious Bible.

As I listened to the story, I had chills all over, and I kept hearing God say, "I am faithful to those who follow My voice." I was so excited to be part of God's huge plan. Thank You, God!

Jeff sent my treasured Bible back, but now it was worn and well read. It means even more to me now than before, because the treasure I lost became the treasure that saved the lost. Don't we serve an amazing God?

A Tiny Handful of Promise

NORRIS BURKES

I t was 3 A.M. when the doctors flooded her room with light. Still numb from pain medication, the new mom fumbled for her glasses, squinting to distinguish the blur of white coats. The doctors were saying something about needing some papers signed—now.

Twenty miles and twenty minutes away, a high-pitched beep suddenly filled my dark bedroom. Numb from the early hour, I fumbled for my glasses, too, so I could read the number on my pager. "Oh no, it's too early," I groaned, even as I shuffled toward the closet where I had pre-positioned my clothing. Still groggy, I managed to get dressed while placing a whispered phone call to the maternity ward.

"Chaplain, we have a baby who's not doing well," the nurse reported. "The parents are asking for you to please come."

Maternity wards are the happiest places on earth—except when they are the saddest places on earth. The contrast in patient stories on the floor can be jagged and capricious. Even as I enter a room of sobbing parents, I often will glance over my shoulder to see other families happily backslapping each other with congratulatory pats.

As I stepped to the bedside, the couple told me of their journey through a problem pregnancy filled with frightening neonatal reports. Nevertheless, they had nursed thin hopes that doctors would find things more fixable than predicted. But now the baby had arrived, and initial reports showed underdeveloped lungs and a leaky heart that was beginning to fail. Concerned doctors were seeking parental consent for a birth-day surgery.

"Has God just teased us?" the parents wondered aloud. "What do we have to do? How do we pray? What do we say? Would it help to baptize the baby? Can you baptize her, Chaplain? Or bless her? Something. We've got to do something! She's got to have a chance."

Now, you have to understand: in my tradition I don't baptize babies. But those who would argue theology at a time like this have never looked into the eyes of desperate parents and heard them say, "Do something, Chaplain!"

I asked the mother if she might have the strength to come with me to the neonatal intensive care unit (the NICU, which staffers pronounce "nick-u"). The NICU is a world of wires, IV bottles, tubes, and back-lit beds that remind me of the scene in the movie *E.T.* when scores of scientists and doctors examine the little alien. In close quarters, the doctors, nurses, and respiratory therapists squeeze through tangled tubes to deliver highly specialized health care to the tiniest people you'll ever see. But as cramped as it was in there, the staff made room as I entered with parents and two sets of grandparents in tow. As we encircled the baby, the usually noisy NICU fell silent in readiness for this "emergency blessing."

Mom stood beside her tiny daughter, stroking the baby with her index finger in an attempt to reestablish the sustaining love of the umbilical cord. Her finger seemed just long enough to maintain a fragile connection between her and this baby of faith. It was an image reminiscent of the fingertip touch between God and Adam in Michelangelo's painting in the Sistine Chapel.

In the *E.T.* movie, special-effects artisans attempted to recreate the scene using an extraterrestrial with a flashlight finger to deliver a healing touch to a child, but Hollywood could never paint *this* scene. Yet it is a scene that is enacted every day in our special-care nursery.

Here was a mother trying to give her very breath to a child who could only breathe with a machine. With the touch of a single finger, Mom was sharing the hopes and prayers of a family.

Unceremoniously opening a bottle of sterile water, I placed a drop on the baby's forehead and asked that God "bless this child in the name of the Father, Son, and Holy Spirit."

With that, Mom's whimpers melted into weeping. And as she cried, she took her daughter's tiny hand and, finding a spot that wasn't wrapped, poked, or monitored, she placed a kiss in that tiny palm and whispered something into those little, curled-up fingers. Then, as if she had placed a thing of priceless value in her daughter's grip for safekeeping, she closed it tight.

This mother's love reminded me of the miraculous way in which God whispers His love into the hand of each of us when we are born, placing there a promise that, no matter what, He will never let us go. And having pledged that love to us from our first breath to our last, He wraps our fingers around that promise for safekeeping.

The apostle Paul wrote, "For I am persuaded, that neither death, nor life, nor angels, nor principalities, nor powers, nor things present, nor things to come, nor height, nor depth, nor any other creature, shall be able to separate us from the love of God, which is in Christ Jesus our Lord" (Romans 8:38–39 KJV). Even as a minister, I sometimes forget how personal and deep God's love is for each of us. I often talk about the depth of God's love, but it took a mother's heartfelt whisper into a tiny hand to remind me that God is always there to love me, and all I need to do is reach out and accept it.

I'll never know the exact words this young mother entrusted to her daughter's grip. But in the coming weeks of miraculous procedures and risky surgeries, the real miracle that was witnessed by all who would see it was how this little girl never released the grip of her mother's promise.

Three months after her birth, she went home a healthy little girl.

Naturally Supernatural

G. SCOTT SPARROW

I fell down a flight of stairs and was injured so badly that my lower spinal column was in almost constant distress and pain. I had frequent chiropractic treatments for it. Getting in and out of bed became a careful process, and I would be somewhat stiff in the morning getting up. Even so, I rose at 6:30 A.M. for meditation (because it was the least interrupted, quiet time for me) and to prepare breakfast for my husband and children.

This was the pattern of my life for seven years. One evening, my husband stayed up to watch a late TV sports review and I went to bed. I had just changed into my nightgown when I sensed a presence standing close beside me, on my left, and a (male) voice said, "This night, sleep on your stomach." The voice spoke to me as clearly and normally as when two persons are in conversation.

I started to protest in a gentle way. "But you know I can't sleep on my stomach!" I said with mock alarm, meaning that my back would become so rigid in the night that I would need help to get out of bed. Yet even as I said this, I obeyed as quietly as a child would and remembered thinking how astonishing that I could do this, and fell into a deep sleep in this manner almost immediately.

Later, in reliving this extraordinary scene in my mind (and I did many times), I recall how amusing it seemed to me—as I was speaking the words—that I would remonstrate with a spiritual being! It still does. It is recounted here as it happened to illustrate how natural the entire incident seemed.

In the morning, just before actually waking, I distinctly felt the touch of hands massaging, manipulating, and pressing lightly on the lower region of my back. I slipped out of bed as though there had never been an injury.

For three full days I was in a silent, prayerful state filled with awe and reverence, consumed with wonder. Whose hands had I felt on my back? Who was it who had healed me?

On the third night, I went to bed a little earlier again. As I closed the door, the entire wall facing me disappeared, and where there had been a large window and tall furniture occupying that wall space, there was now a brilliant panel of light. I stood transfixed, gazing at it. In the center was a figure in full height, with his hands outstretched, palms upward. He was showing me how my back was healed and who had healed me. I say "he" because I knew instinctively it was the voice I had heard earlier, but this time no words were exchanged. The figure appeared to be androgynous, neither male nor female, nor were the hands characteristic of either. The face was so luminous I could not make out the features, but the hair was plainly visible. It glistened with soft brown waves and fell to the shoulder. He wore a single white garment with no apparent seams, reaching from the neck to the floor and covering the feet, with full, open sleeves at the wrist.

He stood like this for several seconds, and then the wall reappeared in the fraction of a moment as inexplicably as it had disappeared moments before. I remained in that state of grace for some time afterward, and even today, more than thirty years later, the event is indelibly etched in my mind and very simple to recall in all its detail.

I Come to the Garden Alone

CHRISTINE E. COLLIER

Gardening was one of my mother's favorite pastimes. As a busy mom of eight, her garden gave her a brief escape from everyday problems. It was no surprise that the hymn "I Come to the Garden Alone" was one of her most beloved.

My mother had twins when she was forty-four. Cara was a beautiful baby girl and Chad, a precious baby boy, with some medical problems. Chad was also diagnosed with Down syndrome. They joined six other children in my family.

I am the oldest of this brood and already married with children of my own when the twins were born. My father learned the patience he lacked in his youth with Cara and Chad and spent many happy hours with them. Sadly, he developed cancer and died when they were twenty.

Cara married and started her own family, as did all the other children. Chad remained with Mom. After my father's death, my mother faced severe loneliness and depression. Sometimes she was angry and questioned why she had to have the burden and work of Chad in her so called "golden years." However, countless times she remarked that God surely knew she had to have meaning to her life to keep on going. Caring for Chad gave her that meaning. "He's the only reason I get up in the morning," was a statement she made often. Many times she said to me with full confidence that Chad would be a great man in heaven, a leader of many.

One of Chad's favorite possessions is his CD player and Christian CDs. He loves to sing along to hymns. His distinct voice and way of singing touches your heart. He often sings just the last few words of each sentence. Much of the time he simply hums the song.

My mother died peacefully in her sleep a few years ago. Although tired, often sick, and discouraged, my mother never gave up. She cared for her son until the day she died.

During her funeral, after our pastor's eulogy, we were bowed in prayer when the hymn "I Come to the Garden Alone" began playing. All of a sudden, someone with a rather raspy, strange voice started to sing. The singing seemed to echo in the big, quiet room. It took everyone by complete surprise. Was this a planned event? Why was the singer still sitting with the rest of the guests? Why didn't he stand up or go to the front of the room? No one had introduced a singer. The way the song was sung was far from typical but yet it brought tears to almost every eye. It was Chad, singing in his most unique manner to a song he couldn't resist. Chad knew nothing about the etiquette of public singing. He simply wanted to sing. My heart soared, and I believe it was a sign from God that He was with us. Chad's innocent tribute to the mother who had cared for him unceasingly was done in the most humble and perfect way only God can orchestrate.

Our pastor's voice cracked with emotion when he spoke of Chad during the funeral service. He knew what Chad meant to our mother and all of us. He also had his own personal reasons for this emotion, which he shared with the guests. "My wife and I had our fourth daughter this past fall and she, too, has Down syndrome."

The Tattooed Stranger

SUSAN FARR FAHNCKE

He was scary. He sat on the grass with his cardboard sign, his dog (actually his dog was adorable) and tattoos running up and down both arms and even on his neck. His sign proclaimed him to be "stuck and hungry" and to please help.

I'm a sucker for anyone needing help. My husband both loves and hates this quality in me. It often makes him nervous, and I knew if he saw me right now, he'd be nervous. But he wasn't with me right now.

I pulled the van over and in my rear-view mirror, contemplated this man, tattoos and all. He was youngish, maybe forty. He wore one of those bandannas tied over his head, biker/pirate style. Anyone could see he was dirty and had a scraggly beard. But if you looked closer, you could see that he had neatly tucked in the black T-shirt, and his things were in a small, tidy bundle. Nobody was stopping for him. I could see the other drivers take one look and immediately focus on something else—anything else.

It was so hot out. I could see in the man's very blue

eyes how dejected and tired and worn-out he felt. The sweat was trickling down his face. As I sat with the air-conditioning blowing, the scripture suddenly popped into my head. "Inasmuch as ye have done it unto one of the least of these, my brethren, so ye have done it unto me" (Matthew 25:40).

I reached down into my purse and extracted a ten-dollar bill. My twelve-year-old son, Nick, knew right away what I was doing. "Can I take it to him, Mom?"

"Be careful, honey." I warned and handed him the money. I watched in the mirror as he rushed over to the man, and with a shy smile, handed it to him. I saw the man, startled, stand up and take the money, putting it into his back pocket. *Good,* I thought to myself, *now he will at least have a hot meal tonight.* I felt satisfied, proud of myself. I had made a sacrifice and now I could go on with my errands.

When Nick got back into the car, he looked at me with sad, pleading eyes. "Mom, his dog looks so hot and the man is really nice." I knew I had to do more.

"Go back and tell him to stay there, that we will be back in fifteen minutes," I told Nick. He bounded out of the car and ran to tell the tattooed stranger. I could see the man was surprised, but nodded his agreement. From my car, my heart did a little flip-flop of excitement.

We then ran to the nearest store and bought our gifts carefully. "It can't be too heavy," I explained to the children. "He has to be able to carry it around with him." We finally settled on our purchases. A bag of "Ol' Roy" (I hoped it was good—it looked good enough for me to eat! How do they make dog food look that way?); a flavored chew-toy shaped like a bone; a water dish, bacon flavored snacks (for the dog); two bottles of water (one for the dog, one for Mr. Tattoos); and some people snacks for the man.

We rushed back to the spot where we had left him, and there he was, still waiting. And still nobody else was stopping for him. With hands shaking, I grabbed our bags and climbed out of the car, all four of my children following me, each carrying gifts. As we walked up to him, I had a fleeting moment of fear, hoping he wasn't dangerous.

I looked into his eyes and saw something that startled me and made me ashamed of my judgment. I saw tears. He was fighting like a little boy to hold back his tears. How long had it been since someone showed this man kindness? I told him I hoped it wasn't too heavy for him to carry and showed him what we had brought. He stood there, like a child at Christmas, and I felt like my small contributions were so inadequate. When I took out the water dish, he snatched it out of my hands as if it were solid gold and told me he had had no way to give his dog water. He gingerly set it down, filled it with the bottled water we brought, and stood up to look directly into my eyes. His were so blue, so intense and my own filled with tears as he said, "Ma'am, I don't know what to say." He then put both hands on his bandanna-clad head and just started to cry. This man, this "scary" man, was so gentle, so sweet, so humble.

I smiled through my tears and said, "Don't say anything." Then I noticed the tattoo on his neck. It said, "Mama tried."

As we all piled into the van and drove away, he was on his knees, arms around his dog, kissing his nose and smiling. I waved cheerfully and then fully broke down in tears.

I have so much. My worries seem so trivial and petty now. I have a home, a loving husband, four beautiful children. I have a bed. I wondered where he would sleep tonight.

My step-daughter, Brandie, turned to me and said in the sweetest little-girl voice, "I feel so good."

Although it seemed as if we had helped him, the man with the tattoos gave us a gift that I will never forget. He taught that no matter what the outside looks like, inside each of us is a human being deserving of kindness, of compassion, of acceptance. He opened my heart.

Tonight and every night I will pray for the gentle man with the tattoos and his dog. And I will hope that God will send more people into my life to remind me of what's really important.

The Legacy of Prayer

HOLLY BAXLEY

We gathered in a circle around her as she sat on a mahogany dining room chair. Many hands were laid on her head and shoulders as my sister and I knelt on the floor in front of her and held her gentle hands. We were praying over her because we found out her cancer was terminal.

While others petitioned God, I opened my eyes, stealing a glance at this precious woman, sitting so demurely. Tears trickled softly down her cheeks, but not from pity or anger. I knew that the last person she would ever cry over would be herself. Her sorrowful, heartbreaking tears were over our pain and grief, not her own.

Even though her eyes were closed, she must have felt me glance at her, for she gently withdrew her hand from mine, and placed it on my head and stroked my hair. The tears that I had tried to choke down turned into a sob. So I buried my face in my mother's legs.

Those who had been praying for her stopped momentarily. It was too much for all of us to take in.

And that's when Mom began to pray and thank God for each of us in turn.

As I listened to her, a relieving peace entered my heart. And it seemed I was not alone, for those gathered around her were experiencing the same tranquility. My grandmother was no longer shaking, and my sister was smiling through her tears, nodding her head in agreement as Mom prayed.

After the prayer time was over, my mom looked down at me, still sitting by her feet on the floor. I managed a wobbly smile, as I couldn't trust my voice. It would have betrayed my feelings. I looked behind her to the row of pictures on the fireplace mantle. My eyes settled on a picture of a smiling high school couple. The young man stood close to his date wearing a black tuxedo with bow tie and cummerbund that matched the young lady's southern belle formal.

As Mom looked toward the picture, too, her eyes brightened. "I'll never forget the day I bought you that dress. Wasn't that amazing? How good God is to us!"

Wrapping her arms around my waist, she gave me a strong hug, despite her fragile condition. And we reminisced about the day the dress came our way.

It was a week before the Junior/Senior Banquet and I was feeling dejected. I had been searching for a formal to wear, but due to our budget on Mom's single-parent income, an affordable one was not anywhere to be found. Sensing my discouragement, Mom read from one of our favorite passages, Psalm 37. She told me that God took great pleasure in delighting our hearts, even in the small things in our lives. She said, "We're going to pray that God leads us to the perfect dress for you!"

"But isn't it more important to pray for God to meet our needs?" I countered. "This is more of a want than a need."

She cheerfully replied, "You may see this as a *want*, but I see this as a *need* for you to know that God will provide for you."

She grabbed her prayer journal and jotted down the date and the request that God would provide a dress for me. And then we held hands and prayed. She went to sleep confident that God would honor our prayer. And I went to sleep feeling guilty for praying for a dress.

The next afternoon she asked me, "If money were no object, what kind of dress would you like to have?" I explained the style to her, to which she replied, "Could you draw it for me?"

I drew a southern belle type of dress, with ruffles across the top and bottom and explained that I wished it had a bustle in the back with a long silk sash around my waist.

She stared at it and asked in a voice that trembled, "What color would you want this dress?" "Sky blue," I replied.

And with that announcement, her eyes opened wide as she exclaimed, "Wait right here!" and she bounded out of sight.

A couple of minutes later she was back, flinging something in my arms. It was a beautiful sky blue formal in the exact style that I had just drawn!

"Go try it on!" she urged. It fit perfectly. "You know what the best part is?" she beamed.

"What?" I asked incredulously.

"I got it for five dollars from Goodwill."

She shared how during her lunch hour, she felt impressed to stop by Goodwill and see what they had. On a rack toward the back, she spied it. "I knew in my heart that this was the one. And to think, we even have your drawing to confirm it! God provided for us, Holly! I told you He would give you the desires of your heart. All we had to do was pray in faith."

Pray in faith. That had always been the heart of my mother's life. Whether it was to pray for a dress for her daughter, or to pray for the salvation of a friend, she never wavered in her belief that God would come through. He always had and He always will.

As she continued to hold her arm around me as we looked at that snapshot of His faithfulness from the past, she whispered, "You will always know of God's faithfulness and love, because I've prayed that over you. It's written in my prayer journal, and I know it will continue to be answered each and every day."

Now sixteen years after her death, I continue to write in prayer journals of my own. Recently, my four-year-old daughter snatched the current one off my nightstand. She held it up. "Mama, whaz this book?" And as we snuggled together, I explained the legacy her grandmother had left for both of us.

Something Extra

DOROTHY CLARK

D orothy, we're in a terrible pinch," a woman explained to me over the phone one day. "The regular teacher for one of the special classes cannot be with us this Sunday, and we have no one to teach these students. Could you possibly help us out at least this once?

I recalled the classroom scene I had seen several weeks before—the hunchback woman bellowing out coyote howls, the oversize boy stretched out on the stage kicking and screaming, the young girl talking out loud to herself during the lesson, and the constant noise and interruptions.

How could a teacher possibly keep order? I asked myself. *And what in the world could I possibly tell those students that would make any real difference to their lives?* But I remembered the prayer time that had followed and the childlike trust I had observed. Maybe they could be taught.

"Dorothy, are you there?" prompted the lady on the phone.

"Yes, and, well, I can't promise you much, but if you

need a teacher that badly, I'll . . . I'll try to help out," I heard myself saying.

For several years my church, Walnut Creek Presbyterian in Walnut Creek, California, had been holding a morning worship service for the mentally and physically disabled. I knew of the church's need for workers, and I had even felt that perhaps this was where God wanted me, but I didn't feel ready to take on an assignment like this one.

Several times I'd been asked to help. "Lord," I had prayed, "I'll do anything but that." But the need was too great and the call too persistent to deny it any longer. Now, finally, I had consented to go, but just for one Sunday.

As I entered the class, I saw cerebral palsy cases, childlike mentalities in adults' bodies—about thirty mentally challenged individuals, ranging from ages six to sixty-five. They were together in the church fellowship hall, a large room complete with a stage and sound equipment.

As I nervously glanced around, the face of one young boy stuck in my mind. His name was David, and he had cerebral palsy. I couldn't help wondering if our son would have been just like him if he had lived. (I was five months pregnant when a miscarriage disclosed the premature signs of deformity in our dead son.) And then I remembered the premature births of our other five children—all dead.

So, we had adopted two children and our home couldn't have been happier until our little girl incurred a rare bone disease. As that two-year ordeal came to a close and little Carrie emerged intact, our young boy, Ron, was taken down with rheumatoid arthritis. The agony of seeing my boy in such severe pain, that at times he would ask God to let him die, was almost more than I could bear. Then after seven years, God healed the humanly incurable condition. Ron was twelve at the time, and today he is a healthy, normal young man.

I'd had my share of illness too. Cancer, starting in the thyroid, had spread, requiring numerous operations. It seemed I was always in difficulty. Robbed of the right, so I thought, to normal living, I felt of little worth to God or anyone. And each time I or one of the children was taken from the mainstream of living, I had to face a new resistance within.

Through it all, I had learned that there is no such thing as a right to normal living. When it comes to physical, mental, or spiritual levels, God has made us each unique to fit His purpose. I had discovered also that it was not the problems, but my reaction to them that determined my success or failure.

I learned to thank God for every situation, believing that God allowed it for a purpose. I learned to look for blessings from my trials. And I learned that one's worth is not determined by one's physical or mental assets, but by one's willingness to be at God's disposal.

Now, as I faced this roomful of special people, I wondered, *Did God intend my trials to prepare me to work with these disabled ones?*

"Now, it's time for prayer," said one of the women. The students, in groups of eight or nine, went to smaller classrooms to pray. What would they possibly pray about?

The prayers were short—a thank you, a remark about the flowers or trees. But as they prayed around the circle, I had trouble keeping back the tears, because without exception, each one thanked the Lord for sending "Dorothy" to them.

God was preparing me for the next step, because I was very soon asked to teach the entire class. I prayed, "Lord, maybe I can't do much, but You can. I'm going to ask You for a small miracle. Please keep the room in order while I tell them about You." And then an idea flashed, "In fact, Lord, I'm going to make that the test. If You really want me to help these students find You, keep them perfectly quiet during the lesson."

It was a faith-venturing Sunday. During the preliminaries the students were more unruly than at the previous session, including the boy sprawled on the stage.

"Lord, I'm trusting You," I prayed. "I've left it in Your hands. I've asked You to keep the classroom absolutely quiet while I teach. That's our agreement. And please, Lord, can't You get that boy down off the stage?"

As I rose to speak, an idea hit me. Pulling the blackboard over just a few feet put a barrier between the boy and the class. Unable to see what was happening, the boy soon forgot his bellowing and, without any assistance, came down off the stage and sat quietly.

"Shall we all bow our heads and our hearts before the Lord to worship Him," I began. Chairs shuffling, coughs, giggles—I waited with head bowed. Within a few minutes, thirty mentally and physically impaired students had quieted. And they remained without so much as a whisper as I told them about a loving heavenly Father who could meet their every need.

"Mrs. Clark," the school's principal spoke up after the class. "in all my years of working with the special students I have never seen anything like what I've witnessed today. Would you consider teaching on a permanent basis?"

"But I'm not a teacher," I said, laughing. And with a glance at his startled expression, I added, "But if you want to know, it was the Lord who made the difference in class this morning."

That's how it all started. I wasn't so sure I wanted the job, or that I could handle the situation, but I made the decision to trust the Lord. God, Himself, helped me with my fears by giving me something extra.

The Message of Bubbles, Flowers, Raindrops, and Leaves

BETTY BEAVER CANTWELL

The subtle wonderment of soap bubbles disappearing in the air, the naive appreciation of weeds, or the enchantment of sunlight streaming through wet leaves—my grandson, Jack, has been blessed by a series of everyday miracles.

Years ago, when I saw Jack as a newborn in the hospital, he had needles, lines, and tubes attached from his head to his toes. When I picked him up it was like gathering a floppy rag doll. I felt sorry for him. I prayed that he would survive.

The doctor said Jack had Down syndrome. We were stunned. Questions hounded us. "Why? How did this happen? Was it possible that the doctor was wrong?" Jack's great-grandmother, not understanding Down syndrome, said with confidence, "He'll outgrow it." We were dedicated Christians and believe that all things worked together for good, but how could good come from this?

When he was a few months old and other children his age were sitting alone, Jack's mom propped him up beside his cousins. Blonde, cute, and cuddly, he promptly toppled over. We wondered if he would ever be able to sit up by himself. Eventually, he did. As he grew, every new achievement was a miracle in itself—his first awkward steps, his self-feeding, and his first night sleeping without wetting his bed.

After attending a party with other parents and their Down syndrome children, Jack's dad commented, "Jack just sat at the table and ate his cookies, while other kids played and chased each other. He didn't pay attention to the other kids." We wondered if Down syndrome might not be his only challenge. Four years later he was diagnosed with autism. This explained some of his behavior—his lack of eye contact, his screaming when tires hummed on the highway of a curving road. When cutting his hair, Jack's mom used scissors because he couldn't stand the buzzing sound of electric clippers. A barber was out of the question.

Jack had a passion for soap bubbles long before he was able to blow his own. With his chubby little hand he dipped the wand in the jar and swished through the air. A trail of bubbles floated away and disappeared over the backyard fence. Each time he was amazed with the creation of the bubbles. He watched as the wind lifted and turned them, and was always surprised when they disappeared. He did this for hours. After he learned to blow bubbles, Mom kept a generous supply of jars on hand. One day Jack went missing from the yard. Mom found him minutes later several blocks from home, a trail of bubbles following him. Traffic stopped as he attempted to cross a busy boulevard. Mom quickly parked her car and chased after him. "What are you doing?" she fussed at him as she grabbed his hand.

"Na's house," he replied. He obviously knew the way to Nana's, and if the streets hadn't been so busy, he might have made it. It was a miracle he was found quickly and unharmed.

While he enjoyed his bubbles, Jack also liked to keep Mom company when she worked in the yard. One day he entertained himself with his bubbles while she pulled dandelion weeds from the flowerbed and put them in piles. After pulling the weeds, she set out a bed of rose moss and went inside to put the laundry in the dryer. After a while, she looked out the window and saw Jack pulling up all her newly planted rose moss. He put them in neat little piles as Mom had done with the dandelions. As Mom came running into the yard, he clapped his hands and hollered, "Yea!" as if he had accomplished something wonderful. Perhaps to Jack, they were all flowers—he just hadn't figured out whether they should be planted or pulled up.

Getting ready for school each morning was a ritual. Jack was not one to be hurried, and getting dressed could be a chore. He looked smart in his new glasses. A hearty eater, he enjoyed breakfast whether it was a bowl of Cheerios, which he called Os, or scrambled eggs, sausage and biscuits. His morning medication had a calming effect, and if he missed a dose everybody knew it. Mom packed a lunch of chicken nuggets, fruit, chips, and a drink. His lunch box went into his backpack. All this had to be done before the bus honked.

Jack's mom had been in the habit of holding his hand and walking him to the bus. When Jack turned ten, Mom encouraged him to be more independent. She allowed him to walk from the front door to the bus by himself. For one week, he did fine. He went out the door with his backpack, walked down the sidewalk and climbed into the waiting bus. Mom waved to him and they both looked proud.

One morning, the bus was early and Mom was still in her nightgown.

"The bus is here!" Mom called out.

"Bus," Jack repeated in his typical one-syllable answer. Mom helped him with his backpack and let him out the door.

"Go on, Jack, go," she called to him from behind the door, her head sticking out.

Jack lumbered toward the bus. A lingering raindrop, left over from the morning shower, fell onto his hand. He stopped in the middle of the sidewalk and inspected the drop of water. He looked at the overhanging leaves, expecting another raindrop to fall. The shining jewel-like drops clung to the leaves. Sunlight danced through them, sprinkling rainbow colors.

"Go, Jack, go!" Mom urged. Jack examined his hand. The raindrop had disappeared. He studied the branch of jewels and waited for another to fall into his palm. The bus driver waited, but he couldn't wait much longer.

"April, come quick!" Mom called. "Help Jack on the bus." April, Jack's seven-year-old sister, ran past Mom barefooted, but otherwise fully dressed. She would leave for another school in a few minutes. She saw the problem.

"Walk, Jack, walk," April told him. She leaned on him. But Jack was enthralled with something else: the beauty of sunlight streaming through wet leaves, a heavenly garden of God's own creation where raindrops glistened like jewels, and brilliant colors sparkled in every drop. He rocked from one tiptoe to the other, humming contentedly. Never mind that the bus waited for him. Never mind that Mom called to him from the doorway. Never mind that his sister leaned on him.

"Go to the bus," April said. Jack took a step and stopped. April pressed her hands against his back. With her head down, like a train shoving a heavy load down the track, she pushed him down the sidewalk all the way to the bus. As Jack climbed into the bus, the driver and his assistant cheered as if he had completed a 50-yard dash. Jack smiled.

I admit it's not easy for me to slow down in this hurried world. Being with Jack teaches me patience and enjoyment of everyday miracles in God's creation. He has me pondering new things—how long does it take a soap bubble that is three inches in diameter to disappear on a calm day? Is rose moss really lovelier than a dandelion? And what about raindrops that sparkle like jewels?

I wonder.

CHAPTER 5

Miracle Messages

Faith comes from hearing the message, and the message is heard through the word of Christ (Romans 10:17 NIV).

God's Word is replete with miraculous messages sent by God into His world. Angels made important announcements, prophets predicted the future, people had revealing dreams, God's own voice was heard from heaven, and even donkeys talked. And God still speaks to us today, if we learn to listen to His divine whisperings.

Wright Is Right

ANITA WADLEY

The phone call came as I was walking the aisles at Target. It was my Realtor telling me that we had a contract offer on our house. This is exactly what I had been praying for. This is what everyone had been praying for. But when it finally happened it was devastating! The sale of my house would mean I was homeless. *Where was I going to go?* For the first time in my life, at age fifty-three, I was facing having to make a decision of where I was going to live. *How was I going to live, in the midst of an unwanted divorce, after thirty-three years of marriage?*

I drove straight home and spent the evening in tears. I cried out to God for direction, wisdom, and comfort. And He was there. During my devotion time the next morning I read from *A Minute of Margin* by Richard A. Swenson. I opened to Day 54 of the reading I had been doing and it said, "If you are not sure, wait. Pray. Pray some more. Ask for godly counsel. Pray some more. Read the Scriptures. Pray some more. Wait. When God speaks, you will hear Him—if your heart is at home."

Nothing felt like it was home, especially my heart. It

was broken. I didn't *feel* like I had a home. But in my head I knew the truth of God's Word. Hebrews 13:5–8 says, "Let your way of life be free from the love of money, being content with what you have; for He Himself has said, I will never desert you, nor will I ever forsake you, so that we confidently say, the Lord is my helper, I will not be afraid. What shall man do to me? Remember those who led you, who spoke the word of God to you; and considering the outcome of their way of life, imitate their faith. Jesus Christ is the same yesterday and today, yes and forever" (NASB). Everything in my life was changing. But God had not changed. He was still with me. As I prayed I sensed God saying, "Wait."

So I spent the rest of the day driving around looking at apartments to rent and writing down numbers from signs in front of rental houses. I came home in tears again, crying out to God, telling Him, *I just can't move into a place that's not mine. I can't have my children come to visit me in a place that is not home. And not only that, Lord, I just can't move twice. I can't. I can't.* I don't think it was pride that was holding me back. I had accepted the fact that I needed to downsize and would need to find something within my budget. It was just a sense of so many changes in my life; I just felt the need to be settled somewhere. I needed a place that I could begin to build a new life for myself and my children. I needed a place that felt like *home!* Couldn't God understand that?

The next day I was with a group of women and one of them gave me a lead on a patio home. My mom and I drove by it and decided it might be a possibility for me. After all, was it coincidence that I was looking for a place to move and this friend knew about this great deal? Maybe *this* was what God had meant when He said, "Wait." Maybe this was it! I called my Realtor and made an appointment to look at the home the next day. As we met and walked in I immediately knew this was not the right choice for me. It was not in a familiar part of town, not the right price, and not the right floor plan for my family. Besides, it just didn't feel like *home*.

I was disappointed and wondered what to do next. As I began to think God brought to my mind another area I had been interested in. Each time I had driven down the street past this addition I had felt God drawing me to it. I had frequently driven through the addition and had walked through a couple of houses under construction. But it had been a while since I had been back.

My mom and Realtor were excited to go back and look with me. We drove up to a house that I had had my eye on and the door was open. The minute we walked in I knew. The colors were what I would have picked. Many homes in this price range have painted white woodwork but this one had natural wood, exactly the color I had picked for the custom-built home I was moving from. The room arrangement would allow all four of my children to visit me at once, and three full baths in a house this size was very unusual. Even the price was right. It would allow me to pay cash with my settlement and not have a house payment. My Realtor said, "Anita, go home and pray about it and call me tomorrow if you want to write a contract." I agreed.

As I was driving home my cell phone rang. My Realtor said, "You won't believe it. There is another couple at that house ready to write a contract right now. The listing Realtor says that if you want to make an offer she will accept yours first since we looked at it first." I pulled over to the side of the road. I was in a dilemma but I wasn't fearful. I had a sense of peace that was beyond under-standing. I remembered the words from my devotion a couple of days before. I had been waiting for God to show me His plan, but I hadn't prayed about this decision yet. *What am I supposed to do?* I said a silent prayer and sensed that it was the right house and the right decision. That's what I had asked God to show me. I called my Realtor back and told her to go ahead and make the offer at the full price.

When she called me to let me know the house was mine, she said, "Go home and pray about it and if you wake up in the morning and you feel sick, just call me and we'll let the other people have it. You won't lose your deposit money. It will be OK."

I dropped my mom off and went home for my nightly walk around the neighborhood. It was a beautiful spring evening in late April. As I started up the street I began to pray out loud. "God, I need to know if this is the right decision. I need to know if this is the right house. And I need to know now!"

As I walked along I heard God speak to my heart. *Tell me the name of your street.* That is what He said. *Tell me the name of your street.* Until that very moment it had totally escaped me. My new address was to be 139 *Wright* Circle.

I began to skip and jump and laugh as I smiled and marveled at my loving heavenly Father and His care for me. I would have many doubts and fears through the months and year ahead, but I have never doubted that that decision was right. It gave me the confidence that I needed to get through all the other tough times. Even now, almost a year after the divorce, when I go through tough times, I look back to that day and know that He cares for me and that He will continue to provide for my needs.

That next morning I opened up my devotion book and Day 59 said, "Fully understand: This is an adventure, not a luxury cruise. But what a joy to feel the pleasure of the Father while humbly traveling the *right road.*"

We can have joy in our lives even in the midst of difficult times when we are walking with the Lord. It is my prayer that I will continue to walk with Him on the *right road*, on *Wright Circle*, until He takes me to my forever home.

Rainy Day Soup

DONNA SMITH

I watched the street turn into a muddy stream. The rain drummed on the metal roof, and bolts of lightning lit up the sky. The phone rang. I took a deep breath and picked up the receiver. *Please don't let it be Mrs. Dodd.*

"Walker's Grocery."

"I need something."

My throat tightened. It was Mrs. Dodd, an eccentric older woman who lived alone with her dog, Daisy, and who traipsed to town three times a day for one-item-at-a-time grocery shopping. Once, I suggested that she buy for a whole day and save herself the four-block walk.

"What's the matter with you?" she had asked, her lips thinning. Her eyes were like pieces of green ice. "Do you think I can carry more than this?" She held up a loaf of bread and a can of tomato soup. "Besides," she said, her mouth softening, "Daisy needs the exercise." Hearing her name, Daisy plopped her front feet on the counter.

I tried not to yell. "Mrs. Dodd, please take Daisy outside. You know the health inspector said that no animals are allowed where food is sold."

She yanked Daisy's leash. "You're not as nice as your husband."

I certainly wasn't. Bill, the ultimate marshmallow, always found a way for Daisy to "shop." He either lifted her into a paper-lined grocery cart so she couldn't investigate the produce or enticed her outdoors with a bone while Mrs. Dodd searched for her inevitable can of tomato soup. Bill also acted as Mrs. Dodd's "business manager." On the first of every month, he cashed her Social Security check and paid her utility bills. In fact, I believe he was ill right now because of having waded in water yesterday to get her mail, deliver her lunch, and take Daisy for a walk. He'd returned, shivering, dripping streams, his shoes squishing muddy puddles.

"Bill, you know you're supposed to be taking care of yourself." He'd recently been diagnosed with early signs of congestive heart problems. "Why do you do this?" I blotted the water dribbling from his hair.

He spoke through chattering teeth. "Maybe someday, if my mother needs help, someone will be there for her."

I winced, remembering my own mother and Bill's mother, both widowed. My mother lived a thousand miles away, but Mama (Bill's mom) lived in the same county, and like Mrs. Dodd, she trekked to town daily for her mail and a can of biscuits. Now, pushing away the image of Mama's blue-veined, slightly bowed legs marching six blocks in rain or shine, I tried to sound friendlier than I felt.

"Hello, Mrs. Dodd. What can I do for you?"

"I need a can of tomato soup."

I willed myself to be patient. "Mrs. Dodd, Bill's home sick, and it's raining sheets. I can't leave right now."

"What's the matter with you? Daisy and I are hungry. If it doesn't stop raining, what will we do?" Daisy barked in the background. I heard Mrs. Dodd shuffling paper. "I'll call Bill. He'll come."

"Don't do that. I'll be there. What do you want?"

"Tomato soup!" she shouted. "Is something wrong with your hearing? And bring a can opener. Mine's broken. Bring Daisy some food too."

Luckily, she hung up before I did. She missed my best ear-piercing slam dunk. Struggling into my jacket, I looked at my low-topped sneakers. Not the best for wading, but southwest Oklahomans don't waste money on rain slickers and boots. Minutes later, clutching soup, dog food, and a can opener, I headed for the delivery truck. Thankfully, some kind soul had placed boards for fording the street-creeks. But in my hurry, I stumbled down the slanted plank and slipped into the rushing, muddy water below.

"Oh-o-o-o, no-o-o!" I lifted my foot. A muddy Styrofoam cup, draped in a thatch of soggy leaves, bobbled on the toe of my bedraggled tennis shoe.

Thunder sounded closer. I had no more than pulled

into Mrs. Dodd's driveway when rain gushed from the sky as though God had emptied tubs of water from heaven. I pushed open the truck's door, sheltering the grocery sack inside my jacket. High-stepping a water-filled rut, I splashed through Niagara Falls to the back steps.

Mrs. Dod spoke through a narrow opening in the back door. "Take off your shoes. Don't track that sludge on my kitchen floor."

Huddled on the small porch under the roof overhang, I scooted out of my limp, wrinkly shoes, pushed my way into the house, and set the sack on the kitchen table.

"I hope you feel better tomorrow, Mrs. Dodd." I turned to leave.

"What's the matter with you?" Her voice quavered like a loose violin string. "Don't you know I'm sick? I can't open that can."

Sighing, I opened the soup and the dog food, then turned again to leave.

"Well," Mrs. Dodd said, "aren't you going to put it in a pan for me? And what about Daisy? She can't feed herself. What's the matter with you? Don't you even care?"

She slumped like a rag doll against the table. Daisy whined at her feet. The question hung in the air, and I felt tears of rage starting to well up inside me. *Please, God,* I prayed silently, *give me patience, and help me to remember that everyone needs love and kindness. If someone isn't acting friendly, it may be because she's hurting inside. Help me to be a bright spot in a gloomy day. I would hope that someone would do the same for my mother or Bill's mother if they needed it.*

I helped Mrs. Dodd into a chair, heated the soup, and poured it into a bowl. Daisy padded beside me from stove to table and back.

"Don't worry, Daisy," I said, scraping her food into a dish on the floor, "I'm not going to forget you." She gulped hungrily, whining deep in her throat.

"Can I do anything else before I leave?" I asked, opening the back door.

"Yes. Take back that can opener. I don't have any more soup." She bent her head over the bowl and, not looking at me, said, "I'll tell Bill you're a good girl."

Wordlessly, I stuck the opener in my jacket pocket. At least next time I'd be prepared. I went out, closing the door gently behind me. A soft rumble from the rain-heavy sky rolled above the treetops. Glancing upward, I half expected God to say, "What's the matter with you? Don't you know everyone in my world needs a little TLC?"

"Yes, Lord," I said, smiling. "Thank you for the reminder."

Startled by a Silent World

NANCY B. GIBBS

I need some time away," I said to my husband, Roy. He was busy with his teaching job. In addition to teaching he was also preaching and coaching. It seemed he didn't have time for me. Our children had grown up right before my eyes and moved away from home. Roy filled his days with activities. I felt lonely and sad. While I was also busy, my life seemed empty. I couldn't find peace regardless of what I tried to do. I needed to hear from God.

There is a little island I have oftentimes called "paradise on earth." I wanted desperately to run away from home and go there. I loved the serenity the beach offered. Even though it was the middle of a cold winter, I knew I wouldn't rest until I visited that place. I would have liked for Roy to go with me, but he couldn't. I needed some time to gather my thoughts and to connect with God, so I decided I would go, even if I had to go alone.

I packed my bags and my poodle's toys, food, and bowls and off we went. Daisey was happy to go with me.

She loved being with me wherever I was. She always had time for her mama. When we checked into the motel, I noticed that I had my choice of parking places. Except for the desk clerk, I didn't see anyone. I had splurged by spending a little extra money and secured a great room with a view.

Later that afternoon, Daisey and I walked on the beach. I looked down the beach one way and didn't see a soul. I looked the other way and, to my amazement, I couldn't see anyone in that direction either. I actually felt a little apprehensive. I had never felt so alone in my entire life.

Daisey and I returned to our room. I pulled out my laptop computer and several uplifting books. I had planned to spend some time writing and reading. I then pulled out my Bible and placed it on the top of my stack of books. I turned on the television. I flipped through the channels, but didn't find anything I wanted to watch.

What will I do for the next three days? I wondered. *This place is even more lonely than home.*

My phone rang, startling me. Roy was calling to tell me he missed me. I realized just how much I missed him too. But regardless, I felt like I had done the right thing by taking the short trip. Our conversation was brief. The second we hung up, I again wondered what I would do. My heart ached for Roy, but I knew he had meetings to attend that evening and the next day. Even if I went home, I would be alone. I was determined to find contentment right where I was.

I spent a few minutes in prayer and began writing again. I meditated on God's Word. In the quietness, I tried to be still with God. But I was startled at the silent world around me. I glanced over at Daisey. She was curled up in the corner of the room sound asleep.

She certainly is a lot of company, I thought.

I was actually glad when darkness fell over the island. It was finally time to go to sleep! Daisey cuddled up with me and we slept soundly that night. We slept late and I missed the sunrise the next morning.

Daisey and I leisurely spent the day together. We took a couple of walks. I ate at a table at the motel restaurant all alone. There were only a few couples in the restaurant. It was during those times that I found that I missed my husband even more desperately.

I longed to go home, but I knew I hadn't accomplished my mission. I continued to pray and to read the Bible. I meditated and wrote. Finally, another day was done and it was time to sleep again. I rejoiced!

The next morning I awoke early. It was cold outside. I wrapped Daisey up in a blanket, threw on some warm clothes, and grabbed the bedspread. We went outside to sit on the porch. It was cold; yet it was also a marvelous experience. I could hear the sounds of the ocean, and when morning broke I could see the waves rushing to the shore. I saw fishing boats in the distance. But I didn't see anyone else.

This has got to be the quietest place on earth, I thought.

Then a burst of sunlight filled the area as the sun arose. I watched the horizon, as if I were watching for a fireworks show. I witnessed a formation of clouds in the sky that brought tears to my eyes. The clouds formed a perfect cross. The rising sun illuminated it. It was then that I finally heard from God. An unexplainable peace fell upon me.

I knew God had used the cross to send me a message from heaven. Tears filled my eyes and I began to pray. For the first time in a long time I didn't feel lonely. God was surely with me. I sensed that I was loved dearly and that God had been with me all along. I realized that He had been waiting for me to give Him some undivided attention.

I don't remember how long I stayed on the porch that morning, but when I returned to the room I knew it was time for me to return home. I looked forward to seeing my husband again. It had only been two nights, but it seemed like a month. My reason for the trip was complete.

"Are you ready to go home, Daisey?" I shouted. When she heard the word "go" she jumped up wagging her tail and searching for her toy kitty.

I quickly packed my clothes and checked out of the

motel a day early. I surprised Roy when I returned home. He grabbed me and held me close to his heart. The short trip did us both good. It made us appreciate each other more.

"The sunrise was awesome!" I shouted. I told Roy about the cross and how God's light shown behind it. I told him how I felt it was a message from God and how it made such a huge difference in the way I felt.

Then I explained the message to him. No matter how lonely we feel, God is always there. No matter how quiet the world is, He is always willing to communicate with us.

My days of loneliness lifted that day. For the first time in a long time my emptiness was replaced with a sense of God's perfect peace and His unwavering love. I have never wanted to run away from home again.

My Own Life Is Proof

DAN WAKEFIELD

I know the truth of Einstein's words; I have lived both ways. Growing up in Indiana in the 1940s I saw the world with wonder, in the frost on windowpanes, in the winter constellations, in the flowers called four-o'clocks that opened around that hour on summer afternoons. Attending Baptist Bible school, I watched in awe as a young preacher and his wife made miracles come to life, using a brown paper bag over a drinking fountain to reenact Moses's drawing water from a rock.

As a young writer living in New York City's Greenwich Village in the 1950s, numbing myself with bourbon and Freud (the former a daily habit and the latter a six-year, five-times-a-week psychoanalysis), I saw the world through a darker lens. With sincere, if self-conscious, cynicism, I adopted an Ernest Hemingway character's prayer of nothingness: Our nada who art in nada. My newfound view of Bible stories was expressed by a pseudo-jaded friend, who had gone to a more enlightened sort of Sunday school, where she was taught scientific explanations of the miracles in the Bible. Just how had Moses led the Israelites across the Red Sea? She explained while exhaling two tusks of cigarette smoke: "Low tide."

Clearly, I was at low tide myself by 1980. Several years earlier I had left my home in Boston and the woman I had hoped to spend the rest of my life with. I had moved to Hollywood to write an NBC series called *James at 15*. Before that, I had worked as a journalist and author for publications such as *The Atlantic Monthly*, *Esquire*, *Harper's Magazine*, and *The Nation*. I had had four novels published, and one of them, *Starting Over*, was made into a movie starring Candice Bergen and Burt Reynolds.

But in Southern California, surrounded by palm trees and people whose satisfaction in life was dependent on Nielsen ratings and box office revenues, I felt things falling apart. When *James at 15* was canceled I stayed on in California to struggle at the entertainment business, constantly drinking to soothe the stress. That created even greater stress and a resting pulse of 120, a condition called tachycardia. I tried to write, but it became impossible. My attention span was getting shorter and my money was getting lower. My life consisted of the nothingness Hemingway's fictional character discovered. Yet mine was real.

I was a few dreary weeks away from my forty-eighth birthday when I woke up screaming one morning. It was more than a nightmare. Wide awake I got out of bed and screamed some more. In misery and despair I groped among a pile of old books and pulled out a Bible I hadn't opened since high school, except for research. I turned to the Psalms, that source of comfort and sustenance to people for more than two thousand years, and read aloud the Twenty-third Psalm.

Throughout the weeks ahead I repeated that psalm again and again. He leadeth me beside the still waters. . . . In the spring of 1980 I got on a plane and returned to Boston, where I went like a homing pigeon to sit on a bench beside the still waters of the pond in the Public Garden.

A new journey for me had begun. I joined a church called King's Chapel and began attending an adult Bible study. I started a steady program of exercise and a healthy diet. By 1984 I was able to give up the constant drinking that had been my addiction—indeed my very identity. But even more amazing, I became free of the desire to drink. The need that had once consumed me was gone, lifted. One of the definitions of the word *miracle* is an extraordinary event "considered as a work of God," and that's how I felt—and still do—about my release from alcohol. There was no doubt: I had experienced a miracle.

Step by step I continued on my way. My minister, the Reverend Carl Scovel, pointed out that the translation of *conversion* in both Hebrew and Greek is "turning." When you turn even slightly you are going a different way, and the further you go the more distant your old way becomes. Instead of a driven, frantic existence, I was gradually changing my perspective, looking inward and focusing on a healthier and more spiritual way.

At the King's Chapel parish house I sat with nine others around a table as Carl Scovel led us in a class about writing a spiritual autobiography. Difficult as it was in the beginning, I slowly began to share my most intimate fears and struggles—and learned that others too had gone through a dark night of the soul. Eventually I started leading workshops myself.

I now saw that a spiritual path really is a path, a genuine ongoing journey, and not just a metaphor. My new path was taking me to churches and adult education centers around the country to guide others in writing their own spiritual autobiographies. I helped people of all ages and backgrounds as they poured out their deepest feelings on paper.

My personal satisfaction was enormous. But by 1993 I was running out of writing ideas—and cash. All spring I had worked on a novel, and when people I trusted told me it wasn't good, I threw it away. "I'm in trouble," I said to a friend. "I need a miracle."

One day not long after, my phone rang. It was a call from an editor in San Francisco. "We've got a great book idea and we want you to write it," he said. What was the subject? Miracles.

"I've got a head start on this one," I told the editor excitedly. I contacted the people I knew from my workshops and asked them to send me stories of what they considered miracles in their own lives.

Next I set out to interview on my own. A woman in Atlanta told me her daughter had suffered a traumatic brain injury when hit by a car and was given little hope for recovery. Yet with prayer from family and friends and Bible study groups around the city, the girl came out of her coma and returned to school and a full life.

A friend in Los Angeles who had suffered third-degree burns and was scheduled for skin-graft operations met with psychologists and medical assistants who were experimenting with alternative healing. The morning after the group had moved their hands above her body in "energy techniques" the burns were gone. (The surgeon who was to do the skin grafts insisted there was no way such a healing could have happened. It happened.)

Rabbi Nancy Flam, one of the founders of the Jewish Healing Center in San Francisco, believes that healing can occur through "the ministry of presence," by clearing one's mind to be fully present to another human being. When we give others our full and loving attention, we become "a conduit for Divinity to express itself." Or, as Thérèse of Lisieux put it in the nineteenth century, "Whose hands are God's hands but our hands?"

In Athlone, Ireland, I met a glowing, rosy-cheeked

woman named Marion Carroll. Others attested to the fact that she had suffered from multiple sclerosis, was blind in one eye, had lost control of her bodily functions, and had been paralyzed in her legs for three years. In 1989 she was taken on a stretcher to a shrine in Ireland. She heard a whispery voice tell her to get up, and when she did, "My legs weren't even stiff!" She hasn't needed a wheelchair or catheter since. "My healin' does not belong to me," she reported. "It's a special gift to people . . . to let them know . . . God's work is happenin' now—like when He walked among us."

But what about people who are not cured? I discovered an even deeper kind of miracle in their stories. Lloyd Kantor, a Vietnam vet who lost both arms and legs and one eye in the war, married and went to Paris on his honeymoon, then took a trip to Tahiti. He and his wife, Loretta, returned to Mount Vernon, New York, to do volunteer work, arranging to have ramps put in the city hall and an elevator in the town library, and to have a memorial erected bearing the names of local men who died in Vietnam. "All in all, things have worked out well," Lloyd told me in a firm, strong voice. "I have to believe it has to do with God."

I discovered that many artists consider their creativity miraculous. While on a visit to Germany, writer Marcie Hershman was dramatically struck by "a silence full of voices still calling out" that reminded her of relatives who had died in the Holocaust, and it led her to write two searing novels about that time, *Tales of the Master Race* and *Safe in America*. "In the Bible, miracles aren't confined just to blessings of joy," Marcie told me. "Some are about evil and how to confront it rather than turn away." Marcie's ability to deal with such a challenge was, to her, a miracle.

Other artists described to me the state of grace they felt on occasions when they transmitted something higher—or what William Blake described as the feeling that his poems were dictated by the angels.

At the same time, we are surrounded by miracles every day. "We see people looking for weeping statues," Frankie Murray, a curate in County Longford, Ireland, pointed out to me. "They miss the every morning miracles—like the sunrise and friendship."

Or the frost on the windowpane in my long-ago Hoosier boyhood. In a sense my path has taken me full circle, back to the simple wonderment at God's mighty hand in the winter constellations. As Willa Cather has written, "Miracles . . . rest not so much upon faces or voices or healing power coming suddenly near to us from afar off, but upon our perceptions being made finer, so that for a moment our eyes can see and our ears can hear what is there about us always."

As for me, I proceed day by day on my journey as a writer and teacher. There is no doubt that miracles abound. The path my own life has taken is proof.

Logic Doesn't Change God's Plans

ISABEL WOLSELEY TORREY

I f you're old enough to remember back to January, 1956, then probably you, also, were in shock when newspapers' headlines blazed, "Five Missionaries Killed in Remote Area in Ecuador." Subheads stated the men's fatalities resulted from having been "Speared by Members of a Remote Tribe." The Woadani (pronounced wow-danni)—initially (but erroneously) known as Auca Indians—were blamed.

Everyone wondered: "How should we respond to this outrage?" Some said, "We should retaliate!" Others, "Let's write off those savages!" What had happened seemed incomprehensible and became the topic of appalled conversations.

However, after the first shock had somewhat worn off, most of us remembered the admonition, "Do not imitate what is evil, but what is good. The one who does good is of God; the one who does evil has not seen God"

(3 John 11 NAS). The widows and their orphaned children decided that in spite of the danger to themselves, they would return to the Woadani nation and demonstrate the power of God's love. It was a tangible way to show, "We practice what we preach." Hundreds who saw their zeal—and also felt a spiritual concern for the sinister tribesmen—pledged their financial support.

Such outgoing response in "returning good for evil," especially impressed a young boy, John, in our church, who added his own opinion: "I'm going to replace one of those missionaries who was killed."

Everyone who'd heard John's intense words, commended him, indulgently patted his blond head and doubtless, like me, mentally dismissed his earnestness with, *Nice thought, but, after all, he's not yet ten years old. He'll have forgotten the matter by spring; certainly by the time baseball season starts. John loves baseball!*

The five slain missionaries, you may recall, were Americans serving with the Wycliffe Bible Translators' organization. Researchers had learned of the tribe's existence and that it was nearing extinction because of constant warring with its neighbors. Those with an apostle's vision reasoned that, if God's Word could be brought to the dwindling survivors, they would understand the futility of killing. And stop.

Getting the Scriptures to these people meant someone must go to—and live among—the Woadani long enough to understand their way of life, learn, then translate their language into a never-before-written language . . . and top it off by teaching them to read. That *someone* must have daring and compassion for Bible-less people . . . and feel an intense desire to go.

What's more, the complicated process would take years. And getting there was another barrier. Obviously, the only way to access the tribe's nearly impenetrable jungle was by air. And—without a runway—it must be done via a plane small enough to settle down in any clearing which might have been chiseled into what appeared as a vast expanse of unbroken heads of broccoli below.

What's more, only a skilled pilot could do such maneuvering.

One of the five dedicated men, Nate Saint, was just such a pilot. Not only that, but he was daring enough to make that kind of an attempt. Yet he and four friends felt a responsibility of taking on such a compelling task.

After buzzing the forested terrain and looking for an opening possibly large enough to eventually land, they found a potential site, but no signs of people.

"They have to be in there . . . somewhere," the men reasoned. "We'll keep coming back. Eventually they should get used to us and maybe show themselves."

Daily, for thirteen weeks, the five flew over the clearing, dropping choice foods and appealing trinkets, hoping that by offering gifts, a friendly rapport would be established.

The idea, which had worked well in other remote

areas of the world, seemed to be succeeding when one morning several Woadani men appeared on the tree-lined fringe. Understandable elation erupted when tribal members responded by putting out their own gifts.

"This is an open invitation. They're letting us know they want us to get together!"

Following a quick touch-down alongside a stream in an open area, a friendly exchange resulted. One tribesman was even bold enough to get into the plane for a quick ride with Nate. It was obvious by his gestures when the two returned, that the awed passenger was describing to his companions how he'd been carried by a "bird."

A mere two days later, however—and without warning—during a subsequent meeting, a small group of Woadani men suddenly speared their "new friends." What had triggered the tribe's seemingly senseless slaughter?

It was during these discussions of "What can I do?" by those back in the States who noted the unselfish efforts of the many who determined to return to the tribal people to demonstrate God's love that the ten-year-old John reiterated his decision.

"I'm going to replace one of those missionaries who was killed." Then he added, "I think it'll be the pilot. Yes, someday I'll be a pilot. I'll take Nate Saint's place."

Years passed. During that interim, translators learned

the language and translated it into print so the people could read Scriptures in their own tongue.

Eventually, a young woman decided the missionaries' message made sense and began convincing others of her people to accept God's forgiveness and great love and stop the killing. She and the translators persisted in their efforts.

Then one day, Mincaye—the Woadani man who confessed he was the one who'd actually speared Nate—approached and asked a long-awaited question:

"You claim God can clean someone's heart. My heart is very, very dark; can he clean mine?" When he was assured the Bible said this is true, he answered, "Now my heart is clear, like the sky, when it has no clouds."

As a tribe leader, Mincaye encouraged others to follow his decision; the killings stopped.

During those years of missionary service by others, I—and the rest of our church members—watched John as he finished grade and high school, participating and excelling in his various, beloved sports, yet never wavering in his desire to become a pilot and replace one of the five slain missionaries. We wondered why he enrolled in an Army ROTC program during college years.

His explanation: "This way I can serve my country and, in the process, learn how to be a pilot so I can replace Nate Saint on a mission field. God will show me where."

I, and others, were appalled when, instead of being commended for putting his experience as a fixed-wing and helicopter test-pilot in Vietnam into becoming a missionary, he received a great deal of criticism, especially from various family members.

His grandmother complained, "Become a commercial pilot instead. They make good money and you could support a family. Besides, with your top-notch grades, plus your experience as a fixed-wing and helicopter test pilot in Vietnam, you could become an astronaut!" (This was during the 1960s when space walks dominated the news.)

His grandfather added, "You've got a wife and two little daughters. Don't risk your life and theirs by going into some remote spot nobody's ever heard of. Probably cannibals live in places like that; they'd just as soon eat you as not. Let those people alone, they're happy the way they are!"

How will John handle this? I wondered. *Will he keep to his goal? Or will he be persuaded otherwise by reasoning? His critics certainly present some valid logic.*

Well, John joined Wycliffe and has spent the intervening years being the missionary pilot he'd planned to become back when he was a ten-year-old boy with a vision for serving.

On the fiftieth anniversary of the tragic event, Nate Saint's son, Steve, supervised the making of a movie,

The End of the Spear, documenting the Woadani story. John was invited to the movie's preview where he met Steve and Mincaye—Steve, the son of the slain pilot and Mincaye, the man who'd killed his father, now not only *friends,* but Christian *brothers.*

Imagine their astonishment when John told the two, "Fifty years ago I determined to become a missionary pilot to replace your father, Steve, the man you, Mincaye, killed."

I learned a profound lesson that day: *God can bring incredible good out of events which, at the time, seem incredibly bad to me.*

I know the above story is true because, you see, John is my son.

Covered with the Word

LINDA SHUBLAK

I awoke early November 30 last year wrapped in romantic thoughts. David and I had been married less than two months, and it was thrilling to open my eyes and find my handsome thirty-five-year-old husband doing his warm-up exercises beside the bed before his daily run. He leaned down, kissed me, and slipped one of his two dog-tag chains around my neck. "Wear these till I come home," he whispered before he left.

David was a major in military intelligence at Fort Huachuca, and as I fingered his tags around my neck, I thanked God for bringing us together. Our marriage was the second for both of us, one we had long prayed about. Each of us had asked God for a lifetime Christian mate, and at last our dream had come true.

I glanced at the clock, jumped up and showered. I had joined a Red Cross class, and was training to become a volunteer at the post dental clinic. Before leaving for class, I wrote David a love note. While I was taping it on the bathroom mirror, where he would see it when he came home to shower, I heard the wail of sirens. I paused to pray for whoever was injured, as I had done since I was a little girl. Then I went off to class, not realizing I had just prayed for my own husband.

I was in class when David's commanding officer appeared at the doorway and motioned for me to come into the hall. One look at his face told me something was wrong. He gave me the news as calmly as he could: "David was hit by a car while he was jogging."

As the colonel walked with me to the hospital adjacent to the dental clinic, I learned that David had been struck by a car traveling about fifty-five miles an hour. The driver had been temporarily blinded by the rising sun, and David had been thrown onto the hood, landing against the windshield. When the horrified driver hit his brakes, David had been catapulted some sixty-four feet and had landed headfirst on the pavement.

When we got to the hospital, medics were moving him onto a flight for the University Medical Center (UMC) in Tucson, seventy-five miles away. I was in a state of shock as the colonel's wife drove me there.

At UMC's emergency room I was told David would be taken to surgery to repair his broken legs and arm. But then a neurosurgeon appeared and canceled those plans. David's head scans showed he had suffered multiple skull fractures, and little brain activity was going on. They would have to put in a shunt immediately to relieve pressure on his brain and use a monitor to gauge his intracranial pressure moment by moment.

The neurosurgeon looked directly into my face. "Your husband is dying," he said. "He has two to forty-eight hours, at most."

I wanted to scream at him or ask if he could be wrong. But I had always been too polite to question people in authority. That's what Holleigh, my twenty-one-year-old daughter from my previous marriage, said anyway. She always tried to get me to stand up for myself. But the doctor was towering over me now. "You should call your family and get them here fast," the neurosurgeon was saying. "And I see your husband marked 'donor' on his driver's license, so you'll need to think about donating his organs."

Suddenly the room seemed to be closing in. I had to get outside. "Thank you," I said. "Excuse me. I have to go pray now." I stumbled to an outside patio and sank down onto a bench. *How can this be happening? How can David be dying?*

My mind escaped to the previous June, to the tranquil front porch of my lakefront house in Sackets Harbor, New York, where David and I had met. I was living a quiet life with Holleigh, and David was on a four-month assignment in the area. I sat reading my Bible on the front porch as David ran by each morning. One day he stopped and started a conversation about the Bible, which led to dating and a proposal soon afterward. We both recognized each other as God's answer to our prayers for lifetime mates.

By the time David's father, mother, and brother, Mark, arrived at the hospital, I was fasting and praying—sometimes silently, sometimes murmuring softly into David's ear while I held his hand—hour by hour. A kind neurosurgeon, Dr. William D. Smith, was now on David's case, but the prognosis was still bleak. When doctors shone a light in David's eyes, there was no response. Soon David sank into a coma.

The pressure on David's brain shot up to five times above normal the next day. Dr. Smith explained that since the brain was swelling and pushing against the skull, circulation was being cut off; my husband's brain was being damaged to such an extent that, if he lived, he would be a vegetable.

Forty-eight hours passed. Dr. Smith told us the monitor showed pressure on the brain that was incompatible with life. "Clinically, your husband is brain dead," he explained gently.

On the fifth day after the accident, when David's condition did not change, well-meaning friends drew up a list of how many of his organs could be used to help those in dire condition. Arrangements were made for David to be buried at Arlington National Cemetery. I understood the others' motivation. I had put my husband in God's hands and would accept whatever happened. But I couldn't shake the feeling that neither God nor I was ready to give him up.

That evening, December 4, Dr. Smith called the family

together. Gently but firmly he explained that we could continue to keep David on life-support indefinitely or we could make the decision to harvest his organs. Holleigh joined us as the family talked it over into the night, our hearts breaking.

When I went to my room, I felt lower than ever. Tears streaming down my face, I took my Bible to bed. God, if David is truly dead and it's Your will that he be with You, I understand. But if there's something more I should do, please let me know.

I opened my Bible to the book of John. And there was the story of Lazarus. I had read it many times before, but suddenly the words took on new meaning. Martha's brother, Lazarus, had been dead for four days when Jesus went to the tomb with Martha. As I read, my tears stopped abruptly. "I am the resurrection and the life," Jesus said. "He who believes in me, though he die, yet shall he live . . . Do you believe?" (John 11:25–26, RSV).

I sat up in bed. "Yes, I believe!" I said aloud. "I believe that if it's Your will, You can save David now just as You saved Lazarus then!"

The next morning I dressed in the brightest-colored clothes I had, as a symbol of life. Carrying my Bible as if it were a sword, I went into David's room to battle for his life. As usual, he was lying spread-eagle on that strangely shaped bed, which moved constantly to stimu-late his circulation.

Maneuvering carefully around all the tubes and medical apparatuses, I started reading the eleventh chapter of John, standing over David's head, then on one side of him, then on the other side of him, and at his feet, even kneeling and leaning under his bed. I was not trying to perform some magical ritual. Rather, I was trying to cover David's body with the Word of God. Doctors and nurses in the room gave me sidelong glances—a few openly disdainful, a few embarrassed, and a few understanding. But I wasn't timid. I read aloud confidently.

When I finished reading, I opened my Bible and laid it on David's chest—the same Bible that had attracted David to me in Sackets Harbor. With my hands on his head, I prayed aloud for a miracle, heedless of the medical people looking on. While I sang "Amazing Grace," David's favorite hymn, his father stood by the window, his hands clasped in prayer, and his brother, Mark, prayed in the chapel. Medical teams came and went.

A neurosurgeon stopped me in the hall afterward. "Get a grip on reality," she told me. "Stop talking about miracles!"

For someone usually so awed by authority, I wasn't the slightest bit intimidated. "Our God is a mighty Healer," I replied simply. All that day when anyone referred to David as brain dead, I was surprised at the authority in my voice when I gave them the same response. Reports of others praying for David bolstered me even more. When I went to the hotel room that night I slept peacefully.

The next day as I walked into David's room, his father met me at the door. "Don't get your hopes up," he said. "But when they examined David's eyes today they saw a flicker of response."

We sat watching and praying at David's bedside. As the hours passed, his arms moved, then later, his legs. On December 7, I wrote in my diary while sitting at David's side: "Buzzers and beeps resound in my husband's room—signs of life to all who hear that Jesus Christ is the Healer!"

Gradually David responded more and more to what was going on around him.

He couldn't talk because he had a tube in his throat, so he wrote notes to his family clustered around his bed. With a shaky hand, he scrawled out to me: "I love you."

The neurosurgeons were all astounded by the reversal of David's condition. They said they had never seen anyone so badly injured return to normal. Dr. Smith said he had never seen a miracle, but he thought he was seeing one now. When the tube was removed from David's throat, he murmured that I was beautiful and asked me to marry him. "We are married," I said, laughing for the first time in days. On December 8, doctors repaired the breaks in David's legs and then his arm. Shortly after, David was moved to the Tucson Veterans Administration Medical Center.

Day by day, little by little, his memory returned—

starting with his earliest behavior and progressing onward. David fast-forwarded in a matter of days from childhood (where he used crayons and played with little cars), through high school and into college (where he sang the Indiana University anthem) to adulthood, where he regained most of his intellectual capacity.

As Holleigh and I helped David get ready to go home on February 2, a new nurse inadvertently placed his legs in an awkward position in the wheelchair. I politely but firmly corrected her, and my daughter smiled. "I'm proud of you, Mom," Holleigh said later. "You stand up for yourself these days."

I fingered the dog tags around my neck, the ones I had never removed. Yes, I had stood up for what I believed in. And now my husband was coming home.

The Miracle Bibles

RON WHEELER

With trepidation, about a dozen people from our church signed up for a two-week mission trip to Guatemala. We began meeting for prayer and Spanish lessons.

Shortly before we left, we were told to try to raise some money to purchase Spanish Bibles to distribute door-to-door. But in the short period of time we couldn't raise much money.

The day before we left, I went to a denominational publishing company to drop off an artwork assignment. (My career is drawing cartoons for Christian publishing companies.) When I arrived, I could barely fit through the lobby as it was piled high with Spanish Bibles! I soon discovered these Bibles had been donated to the denomination for their own mission trip to South America, but the Bibles arrived too late. They didn't know what to do with them. I said, "I have an idea!"

As a result, the denomination gave us two thousand Bibles. Twelve of us spent two weeks distributing them; many of the encounters were miraculous in themselves.

The money we had raised just covered the extra shipping to get the Bibles to Guatemala.

Ironically, I have done work for that publishing house for over twenty years now, and I have never seen (before or since) boxes of Bibles—let alone Spanish Bibles—in the lobby.

As a result of that first trip our church took seventeen years ago, we now have a missions program that sends teams to Guatemala several times a year. We also sent out short-term mission trips all over the globe and now have dozens of missionaries from our church serving full-time with mission agencies around the world.

I don't know how much our involvement in missions stems from those two thousand free Spanish Bibles, but I do know that when the Lord wants to send out His message, He doesn't mess around.

A Transformation
of the Spirit

MELISSA DEAL FORTH

O n January 6 of 1981, my husband, Chris Deal, was diagnosed with acute lymphatic leukemia. At the time, we were living in Nashville.

He had started getting ill before Thanksgiving in 1980. He was a session musician and they played odd hours all the time—their sessions would go on well into the middle of the night. He got in this habit where he started to take naps. He would come home and fall asleep before I could even cook dinner; he was sleeping all the time.

This was strange because Chris was very athletic; he would run five miles a day, but now he just slept, and he began to run a low-grade fever. I tried to get him to go to the doctor, but he wouldn't; he kept putting it off, saying, "Let's wait until after the holidays; it's no big deal."

I believe that Chris knew he was very ill. I think he knew it was serious and wanted to wait until the holidays were over so as not to darken our holidays. I finally convinced him in January to go and see a doctor. We went in to see a general practitioner for a checkup, and I waited for an hour, then two. It was over four and a half hours before I saw him again. I knew that something terrible was going on. When Chris came out, the doctor was with him. The doctor told me then that Chris's white cell count was extremely high and that they suspected leukemia. My heart fell immediately. Chris went to the hospital for more tests, and, indeed, he was diagnosed with acute lymphatic leukemia.

We were told the only way he could survive was with a bone-marrow transplant, so we went to M. D. Anderson, the cancer hospital in Houston, Texas. Back then (in 1981), they would not do bone-marrow transplants unless you were in remission (I understand that now they do so). We had a perfect match in his brother, so basically we were waiting to get Chris back in remission. They were bombarding him with all kinds of chemotherapy trying to get him back, but he would not come back. Several months passed and he became weaker and weaker; it just really turned into a downhill situation for him. It was pretty obvious he was losing the battle.

His room was on the eleventh floor, which was the leukemia floor of M. D. Anderson. The nurses' station is an island in the middle of a round ward. This is so the nurses can see all the patients all the time. Chris had just finished another series of chemotherapy, and his body was really in terrible shape. He was not eating, he slept a lot, he was under a lot of stress, and he was very depressed. He had to have help to just go to the bathroom. After the chemotherapy series, they bombard you with vitamins and a lot of other things to try to keep your body going. At this particular time Chris was connected to two IV poles on either side of his bed. On January 4, 1982, I was sleeping in my cot next to Chris's bed; when laid out for the night, my cot was about eight inches from Chris's bed. Suddenly I was awakened by a nurse shaking me and saying, "We cannot find Chris." She was very upset. I couldn't believe Chris was gone. I was very confused, and I panicked. I jumped up, took off down the hall, and instinctively ran toward the elevators, looking for Chris. All of a sudden I looked and saw the chapel. The chapels are on each floor at M. D. Anderson and they are very small—about the size of a large walk-in closet. There were three sets of chairs on either side with an altar at the back wall, and there's a long glass pane at the entrance to the chapel. I went to the glass pane and looked in. There was Chris and he was sitting with a young man. They were sitting across from each other, knee to knee, and they were talking. I couldn't believe it. I thought, first of all, how did he get his two poles past me and around the nurses' station without being seen? It was also unusual because I usually sleep, as anyone with a loved one in these situations does, with one eye open; I was up if a pin dropped. So I must have slept as if I were in a coma; he managed to get out of that room with two IV poles and not wake me up!

So I couldn't believe he was in there talking to this guy; it was so strange. I opened the door, walked in, and said, "Chris, where have you been? I was so afraid!" And he looked up at me and he was so calm. He said, "It's okay, Melissa, I'm okay. You need to go back to the room." I said, "Chris, what's going on? Where have you been? Everybody's upset; you scared everybody to death!" Just as calmly as could be, he said again, "Melissa, it's okay; you can go back to the room. I'll be back soon; don't worry."

In the meantime, I'm looking at this young man he's sitting across from. Where did he come from at three o'clock in the morning? What was he doing there? I had never seen him before. When I first looked at him, he looked down at the ground, like he didn't want to make eye contact. Immediately I began to check him out, because I was worried; I didn't know if he was dangerous. I noticed that his hands were white and transparent. At one point he did turn and look up at me. Our eyes caught. The only way I can describe his eyes is like ice blue, like huskies, but even clearer than that; he had this light in his eyes. But I wasn't frightened by them. I was mesmerized by them. Then he looked straight through me—no expression on his face. His skin was so white, almost transparent, and there was not one line on his face. I couldn't take my eyes off of him. He looked like a youth, like a teenager, but there was some wisdom, something old about him. The look and the feel that I got from him were not the same.

Then I started really looking at his clothes, and I realized he had on a flannel shirt, Levi's, and lace-up work boots. Chris was a musician, and this was an attire that he wore a lot, and I think, in an odd way, this man was trying to dress in a way that would make Chris feel comfortable. The odd part about his clothes was that they were all brand-new—like they had just come off the shelf. They even had wrinkles in them.

At this point, Chris interrupted us, because I was just standing there, mesmerized by this guy. Chris looked at me again and said, "Please, Melissa, please go back to the room. I'm okay. I'll be back soon." I said, "Are you sure?" and he said, "I'm sure." I was reluctant, but I could tell he really wanted me to leave, so I did. I went back to the nurses' station and told the nurses that I had found Chris in the chapel. They were very relieved. Then I went back to his room and sat on his bed and just waited for him.

I sat there a long time until, about thirty minutes later, he comes. He's got hold of his poles, he's walking by himself, he's smiling, he's energetic, he's strong; it was unbelievable. This man had gone to bed not being able to get up—and yet here he comes, rolling two poles down the hall, smiling. I can't take my eyes off of him; the man that I had fallen asleep with and the man that came into the room were not the same man. When I had seen him before he went to bed, he was a man carrying around the weight of a terminal illness. He was someone who was extremely depressed and his body was physically wiped out by all the medicine they were bombarding him with. The man that came back into the room after he had been to the chapel was like the young, healthy man I had married. He had changed.

I asked, "Who was that guy?" He said, "You're never going to believe me," and I said, "Yes, I will." He said, "He was an angel."

"An angel?"

"Yeah, he was my guardian angel."

He told me—these were his very words—that I was "put to sleep" and he was "called." He said he just jerked awake in his room and had this overpowering feeling to go to the chapel. So he just got up and went. He was spiritual, so I'm sure at points he prayed, but religion was not something we ever talked about. In the chapel, he kneeled down and started praying. The next thing he knew, he heard this voice say, "Are you Chris Deal?" He turned around and that young man was standing there. He said, "Yes, I am."

And the young man said, "Well, I've come to talk to

you." The young man, or the angel, asked him if he had anything he wanted to be forgiven for, and Chris said yes. He wanted to be forgiven for hating his stepfather. He had had a really rough childhood with his stepfather, but he just didn't want to take that hate with him. So the angel told him, "Well, you have been forgiven."

Chris was worried about me, and the angel told Chris not to be worried, that I was going to be fine. That was the word he used—fine. They talked about things in there that Chris didn't share with me; he said he'd rather not discuss them.

At this point, I jumped off and took off down the hall; I wanted to get another look at this guy. But he's not in the chapel, he's not anywhere on the eleventh floor. I go down the elevator. Being a nuclear experimental hospital, M. D. Anderson has real heavy security. Family members have to carry an ID card to get in and out of the hospital after nine o'clock at night. I went down the stairs and there was a security guard at the elevator. I described this young man to him and asked, "Did this guy come down?" He said no, he hadn't seen anybody like that all night. Well, I went back up to the eleventh floor and back to the room, and I told Chris, "No one's seen him; maybe he got off on another floor."

Well, Chris just busted out laughing, like, "Okay, Melissa, if that makes you feel better."

Anyway, that night he slept sounder, more peacefully

than he had slept in months and months. Two days later he died—one year to the day after he was diagnosed. But I spent those two days that we had left with the healthy Chris. Chris had returned to himself. He was smiling, he was eating, he was laughing, he was telling jokes, he was visiting other patients in the ward. It was like he was not sick at all. He had this unbelievable energy; it was like all the weight of the terminal illness was gone. Everything had changed, other than the fact that we were in a hospital; this was the only thing that made us realize that he was sick. He was like he had been when I first married him. It was an unbelievable transformation. When he died two days later, I believe that though Chris's physical body did not survive, his spiritual body was healed. Whatever journey or adventure he was on the threshold of, he really went into it whole, strong, and ready for it. Chris was totally free of all fear, of all pain. Whatever went down in that room that he didn't tell me about, whatever that angel told him or showed him, it took away the pain, it took away the fear. This was a miracle of a different kind.

To all of us, death is so scary because it's final, it's over, it's the end. But that angel gave Chris something that totally changed him, that totally transcended the illness of his body and the depression of his mind.

It was a total transformation of the spirit. He saw something in the future for him that must have been wonderful.

And I've gone on not worrying about Chris; I've been able to go on in life knowing that he still exists, that he is still out there, that he's still . . . alive.

A NOTE FROM THE EDITORS

This original book was created by the Books and Inspirational Media Division of Guideposts, the world's leading inspirational publisher. Founded in 1945 by Dr. Norman Vincent Peale and his wife, Ruth Stafford Peale, Guideposts helps people from all walks of life achieve their maximum personal and spiritual potential. Guideposts is committed to communicating positive, faith-filled principles for people everywhere to use in successful daily living.

Our publications include award-winning magazines like *Guideposts, Angels on Earth,* and *Positive Thinking,* best-selling books, and outreach services that demonstrate what can happen when faith and positive thinking are applied to day-to-day life.

For more information, visit us online at www. guideposts.org, call (800) 431-2344, or write Guideposts, 39 Seminary Hill Road, Carmel, New York 10512.